"Paris is a realist: seeing this conflict is not going to end anytime soon. She is a non-violent peace-maker: knowing we cannot win through the use of force because we are the conflict; we are waging war against ourselves. She is wise: rejecting simplistic solutions and naïve notions. She is a person of faith: believing that as we put away our idols (of moral high ground, institutional preservation, certainty) and instead cultivate faith and reconciling practices we will find paths forward for our conflicted communities and for the Gospel. This is, indeed, Good News."

—MEGAN K. DEFRANZA
Educator, Bridge-Builder, author of *Sex Difference in Christian Theology: Male, Female, and Intersex in the Image of God*, and a co-author of *Two Views on Homosexuality, the Bible, and the Church*

"With clarity, creativity, and compassion, Jenell Williams Paris plumbs the conflict over sexual and gender diversity for the treasures it contains for the Body of Christ: deeper community, spiritual maturity, psychosexual wholeness for all. I am grateful for the wide lens and bold questions she proposes in her commitment to loving Christ and his church. Paris combines anthropological expertise with personal vulnerability and spiritual humility in this deeply encouraging book."

—KRISTYN KOMARNICKI
Director of Oriented to Love, Evangelicals for Social Action

"Both sides in the debate over LGBT sexuality are mesmerized by and locked into the standard, simplistic arguments. Jenell Paris wakes us up to both the complexity and opportunity of the conflict. While the truths she presents don't make the conflict easier, they do make it better. Better because she more truthfully describes the difficulty we are in and therefore helps us make progress toward reconciliation while growing as Christians in the process."

—TIM OTTO
Author of *Oriented to Faith: Transforming the Conflict Over Gay Relationships*, Pastor, Church of the Sojourners, San Francisco

D1490496

"Jenell Paris is a leader—one I follow. Her humble wisdom and the tension she so comfortably lives in compels me to listen and act. Jenell's first book, The End of Sexual Identity, was an early impetus for me to step into the grey space, messiness, and tension where I found Jesus waiting with arms wide open . . . Once again, I find myself deeply moved, challenged, and grateful for Jenell's leadership, voice, life, and friendship. I trust her and I wholeheartedly recommend and endorse her work!"

—ALAN MANNING CHAMBERS
Author of *My Exodus: From FEAR to GRACE*

"The Good News About Conflict transforms our entrenched debates regarding sexuality in the church into hope for Christian discipleship and unity. Paris shows us a tangible way forward that doesn't rely on agreement or conclusions, but instead reframes our posture to lead well in the midst of conflict. This book is truly good news for the church."

—SAMANTHA CURLEY
Executive Director, Level Ground

THE GOOD NEWS ABOUT CONFLICT

The
GOOD NEWS
about
CONFLICT

———

Transforming Religious Struggle
over Sexuality

Jenell Paris
Foreword by Doug McConnell

 CASCADE *Books* · Eugene, Oregon

THE GOOD NEWS ABOUT CONFLICT
Transforming Religious Struggle over Sexuality

Fuller School of Psychology Integration Series

Cascade Books
An Imprint of Wipf and Stock Publishers
199 W. 8th Ave., Suite 3
Eugene, OR 97401

www.wipfandstock.com

PAPERBACK ISBN 13: 978-1-4982-8097-6
HARDCOVER ISBN 13: 978-1-4982-8099-0
EBOOK ISBN 13: 978-1-4982-8098-3

Cataloguing-in-Publication data:

Names: Paris, Jenell.
Title: The good news about conflict : transforming religious struggle over
    sexuality / Jenell Paris.
Description: Eugene, OR : Cascade Books, 2016 | Series: Integration Series |
    Includes bibliographical references.
Identifiers: ISBN 9781498280976 (paperback) | ISBN 9781498280990
    (hardcover) | ISBN 9781498280983 (ebook)
Subjects: LCSH: Homosexuality—Religious aspects—Christianity. | Conflict
    management—Religious aspects—Christianity.
Classification: LCC BR115.H6 P2 2016 (print) | LCC BR115.H6 (ebook)

Manufactured in the U.S.A.   06/20/2016 for James

CONTENTS

Fuller School of Psychology Integration Series

Series editor, Brad D. Strawn, PhD
Evelyn and Frank Freed Professor for
the Integration of Psychology and Theology

The school of psychology at Fuller Theological Seminary began its unique ministry of training clinical psychologists (PhD) in Pasadena, California in 1964. The uniqueness of this training was that it was conducted in a seminary where students received an education that emphasized the integration of psychological theory and science with Christian theology. In 1972 the school of psychology was the first clinical program in a seminary to be accredited by the American Psychological Association. In 1987 it expanded its training to include the Doctor of Psychology degree, PsyD, as well as the department of marriage and family.

In those early days (and in certain quarters even today) some wondered what the two disciplines of psychology and theology could say to each other. Some thought it an contamination to integrate the two conceiving psychology as a secular and anti-Christian science. But the pioneers at Fuller school of psychology disagreed. Rather than taking an adversarial approach, the faculty developed a variety of models for integrative dialogue, conducted empirical research in the psychology of religion, and reflected on working clinically with people of faith. Through it all Fuller has endeavored to bring the best of Christian theology (faith and practice) into honest conversation with the best of psychology (science and practice).

One of the hallmarks of the Fuller integration project is the annual Fuller Symposium on the Integration of Psychology and Theology, better known as the Integration Symposium. Each year a noted scholar working at the interface of psychology and religion is invited on campus to give a series of three lectures. These lectures include three respondents, one from the school of psychology, one from the school of theology, and one from the school of intercultural studies. In this way, the lectures and the dialogue that follows continues in this integrative dialogical tradition.

Included in the *Fuller School of Psychology Integration Series* are works that have emerged from these Integration Symposium Lectures, dissertations projects that have passed with distinction, and integrative projects written by scholars both within and outside the Fuller community. The series endeavors to both preserve the rich tradition of the Integration Symposium as well as create opportunities for new dialogue in the integration of psychology and theology. This volume emerges from the lectures given by invited guest Jenell Paris in February 2014.

Editorial Board:

Laura Robinson Harbert, PhD, Assistant Professor of Psychology, Department of Clinical Psychology

Terry D. Hargrave, PhD, Professor of Marital and Family Therapy, Department of Marriage and Family Therapy

Pamela Ebstyne King, PhD, Peter L. Benson, Associate Professor of Applied Developmental Science, Department of Marriage and Family Therapy

Forthcoming volumes in the series:

Hoffman, Marie T. *A Suffering People: Stories of Trauma and Hope for Evangelical Christians.*

FOREWORD

A lecture with sex in the title will be well attended. At least that is a common observation on campuses today. This proves to be true on seminary campuses as well. Several years ago, then President Richard Mouw of Fuller Seminary addressed the topic of sexuality, including LGBTQ issues, in an open forum on the Pasadena campus. I remember sitting in the overflow room next to other Cabinet members due to the packed auditorium. That evening was not the first of its kind at Fuller, but it did launch a more robust conversation on sexuality.

A subsequent event in Fuller's conversation was the February 18–20, 2015 annual Integration Symposium in Fuller's School of Psychology. Jenell Paris, Professor of Anthropology, spoke on "Courageous Leadership in Christian Sex/Gender Conflicts." Building on her book on the topic, *The End of Sexual Identity*, Dr. Paris extended her thoughts to explore the role of the church and the Christian community in the broader discourse. This book is the product of that series of insightful lectures.

I found the series fascinating on several fronts. Firstly, having an anthropologist from outside our faculty address the psychologists, theologians, and missiologists on the topic of sexuality resonated with me. My doctoral field research in anthropology and urban mission was conducted in the capital of Papua New Guinea. Fieldwork set in Papua New Guinea has played an important role in the history of anthropology, including Bronislaw Malinowski

(1926) on Trobriand Islanders and Margaret Mead (1949) on Manus Islanders. As a young urban missionary and researcher, my own understanding of the varieties of beliefs and practices as they relate to sexuality was greatly expanded by working with migrants from seventeen different tribal groups. Most problematical were the initiation rituals that included sexual experiences with children around the time of puberty. Ironically, the tribal customs that created and governed the sexually demanding rituals were greatly diminished by the lack of social influence in the city, leading to less restriction on sexual abuse.

Secondly, integration as we use it at Fuller brings various disciplines into conversation with our faith. The primary integration at the annual symposium is between theology and psychology. In her lectures, Dr. Paris begins with a contextual reading of Romans 12:1–2 as the introduction to sacrificial living by submitting "our brains, our talking, studying, and thinking, but also our hearts, our souls, and our daily lives . . . in the light of God's mercy." Acknowledging that she was working from the perspective of an anthropologist, she chose to contextualize the turbulence of the current discourse on sex and gender among Christians in the light of reconciliation and discipleship.

For thoughtful Christians, the integrative task requires a range of responses that are both perplexing and satisfying. The current conversation around faith and work is an example. Many business leaders attend church services each week with no expectation of theological reflection on what it means to do business in the contemporary economic climate. So when a biblical scholar or a theologian, such as my colleague Mark Roberts, begins to reflect theologically on business as a Christian vocation, it creates significant interest.

Jenell Paris has the same effect. As an anthropologist, she is adept at creating thick descriptions of culture, clothing issues in the narrative of real people, and telling the story of cultures as living systems drawing on the method of ethnographic enquiry. Her reflection on the first-century biblical passage intersects with relevance into the twenty-first-century narrative on sexuality. Yet the questions she raises are not answered. She is caught in the integrative dilemma. We bring the disciplines into conversation, but we don't reconcile the intrinsic conflicts. As social scientists we are much better at thick description of life together than we are at speaking with theological conviction. The best we can offer is a range of responses, albeit clearly articulated. The challenge is even greater due to the scholarly tendency to stop short of decisive action, leaving the "so what" to the listeners.

Reading the book in contrast to listing to the presentation allowed more time to both appreciate and challenge Dr. Paris's perspective. For this I am very thankful to her for the time spent in producing this volume. I am also thankful because she really doesn't provide the definitive word. This is at the heart of the problem today. Christians are so used to having things packaged that we find an open discourse troubling, even more when the issues are contentious. The result is a tendency to pull into ourselves and draw sharp boundaries around our opinions. The focus is then protecting the boundary rather than dealing with the issues. In essence, we enter the battle because we have territory to protect. One of the interesting contrasts between the Christian communities in the US and other countries is that the sheer size of the faith community affords the oft-exercised privilege of further dividing along lines of ever narrowing views.

Thirdly, as an anthropologist, Dr. Paris struggles with the thought that at some point the theological conclusion may be at odds with the social convention. In some ways this is the antithesis of the observations in my second point. Perhaps it can be said that radical discipleship may require an intolerant position, characterized not by its acceptance of divergent opinions but rather by a strong sense of God's leading toward theological orthodoxy. I hasten to add that I do not find Dr. Paris guilty of unorthodox thought. Rather her challenge to "go meta . . . [so that it] can lift us out of the immediacy of our local context" may in reality be an eschatological hope. We are so embedded in our cultural context that it appears impossible to rise above. Recognizing the challenge of rationality alone, she observes, "It is not our thinking, nor our debating, nor our voting, that will yield holiness. Rather, as we make our whole lives living sacrifices, our minds are transformed so we may discern what the will of God is, what is good and acceptable and perfect." It remains to be seen whether that means full inclusion.

Finally, Dr. Paris has once again used her considerable skills to assist the seminary community to focus on the issues more clearly. It is incumbent upon us to provide space to explore contentious issues drawing at least the contours of both theological and social concerns. In so doing, our graduates are better prepared to face the issues that are anything but tame once they leave the relative safety of the seminary environment. A colleague used to say, "forewarned is forearmed." Obviously not a Mennonite, my colleague was determined to develop leaders and not simply inform participants. As Dr. Paris so aptly challenged us, it is time on the one hand to increase our central commitment to loving others as they are, not as we wish them to be, and on the other it is time to not only to see the social conflict but to realize that righteousness as well as tolerance are virtues in a pluralistic world.

Doug McConnell, PhD
Provost, Fuller Seminary

ACKNOWLEDGMENTS

I am deeply thankful to Fuller Seminary for inviting me to deliver these lectures, especially Brad Strawn, Doug McConnell, and President Mark Labberton.

These lectures began in writing and conversation with The Colossian Forum, a rich dialogue that has shaped my thinking and living. Thanks to Rob Barrett, Michael Gulker, Chris Brewer, Andy Sauer, Tim Otto, Wendy VanderWal Gritter, Walter Moberly, Wesley Hill, and Jonathan Wilson.

Reaching even farther back, these lectures record how my thinking has developed since writing *The End of Sexual Identity*. For shaping my development, I am grateful to Alan Chambers, Gene Chase, Janel Kragt Bakker, Mark Yarhouse, Megan DeFranza, Sherwood Lingenfelter, and Matt Vos. I am thankful to friends at Level Ground, including Samantha Curley, Niko Palacios, and Jonathan Stoner. Gratitude also to new friends at LOVEboldly, including Heidi Weaver-Smith and Nate Collins. Kristyn Komarnicki never fails to inspire me, and her work with the Oriented to Love dialogues (part of Evangelicals for Social Action) puts into practice the ideals described in these lectures.

As always, I appreciate my husband James's support and regard for my writing endeavors, and my young sons' enthusiasm for seeing their mother's name on a book cover.

INTRODUCTION

This book originated as a series of three lectures delivered at Fuller Theological Seminary's 2015 Symposium for the Integration of Psychology and Theology. I was invited because I am an anthropologist with scholarly experience on the topic of homosexuality, but my interest in both the topic and my time at Fuller was far from purely academic. Urgency on LGBTQ issues seems to press from all directions: from within disciplines such as theology, psychology, and anthropology, from within higher education from faculty and students, and beyond the academy from churches, pastors, and laypersons. This is because the issues aren't mere issues; they involve real people in real places with real and urgent concerns. I came to these lectures expecting intense engagement and deep disagreements, reaching beyond scholarly interest to real-world relationships and pressures people face in their churches, families, communities, and within their own lives.

As expected, people disagreed when they entered the lecture hall, and still did when they left. We reached something even sweeter than agreement, however: Christian fellowship and mutual encouragement in faith. We gathered three times, and each time we prayed, read Scripture, and talked and listened. We expressed gratitude. We praised God together. We didn't solve the problem of homosexuality; in fact, we questioned why it is so often framed as a problem to be solved and done away with. Instead, we strengthened our capacity to stay with the issues and the people affected by them, for the long haul.

My deepest hope for this book is that it will offer the same to Christians and churches: deepened wisdom, strengthened stamina, renewed resources for engaging conflict, and a vision for the long haul. No book can give these gifts—people must wrestle these blessings from difficulty themselves, with God's help—but hopefully these words can offer encouragement along the way. I do have a point of view regarding where I'd like to see the church head on LGBTQ issues, but I have an even deeper hope that Christians will live out their deepest values during this struggle. We're a community in tension. How do we live, speak, and act when things are tense? How do we remember and reinforce our communal bonds?

Such are the dreams and questions I brought with me to the symposium lectures, and such were the brothers and sisters in Christ who I encountered there. I welcome you to join in as a reader.

REFRAMING AND RESPONDING

"How should we respond to homosexuals in the church?" Written in large letters on the classroom chalkboard, this question would frame discussion for an hour in my class, an undergraduate gender studies course at a Christian university. A panel of four students had been tasked with developing a question and facilitating class discussion.

The chalk dust hadn't even settled when Michael, a student, raised his hand.

"The whole idea of *response* is dangerous. It makes *them* an issue, or a problem, as if they are passively awaiting our response. They're people. They're us. Your question implies that *we* Christians are heterosexuals, in a position to reach out to *them*, the homosexuals. The way you've asked the question creates segregation and discrimination."

Ian, the student who had written on the board, looked unhappy. "Um, I guess you're kind of right. I'm just saying I think the

Bible is clear in condemning homosexuality, and it seems hard to even say that anymore. Do we have to give up clear biblical teachings just so we won't be called mean?"

Michael replied with frustration, "Well, you're bringing up a whole other can of worms there. What I'm saying is that this whole question, the way you've asked it, sets up a super negative response."

I was a Christian college undergraduate in the early 1990s and returned as a professor in the late 1990s. That time now seems like the distant past, in light of the rapid legal acceptance of same-sex marriage, denominational conflicts and shifts in theology and practice regarding LGBTQ persons, and widespread and sympathetic media portrayals of LGBTQ persons. I remember students reluctant to even utter the word "homosexual" for fear it would mark the speaker as gay, or as overly interested in the subject. Students were hesitant to acknowledge personal association with gays in their families or friend groups. We discussed the safety of touching persons with AIDS, and whether or not gays recruited adolescents into their ranks. In one class a lone gay student spoke up and said, "Hey, let's not assume this issue is all 'out there.' I'm right here." But I don't remember him using words such as *gay* or *homosexual*; he referred to himself as "the elephant in the room."

Today, students readily share stories of friendships and associations with high school classmates, family members, and others in their lives who are LGBTQ. Speaking of one's own sexual minority status is still taboo for many, but increasingly, sexual minority students share their identities as well. I can't imagine a student today asking about touching persons with HIV/AIDS or gay recruitment.

In the past, the issue of homosexuality was just that, an issue out there, disembodied and depersonalized. It was *their* issue, a matter to which *we* responded. *They* were homosexuals, outside the fold. *We* were the insiders, heterosexual believers.

To the question, "Do you believe the Bible says homosexuality is a sin?" *we* would respond, generally with a yes or a no. Either "yes" or "no" could be held with anger and aggression, or with kindness and compassion. Regardless of one's answer, however, and regardless of the quality with which it was held and advocated, the bifurcating question was seen as *the* question. Individuals and institutions declared an answer and joined a side.

Things are changing: we're straining past the limits of these dominating questions. Yet at the same time, things remain the same. Sex/gender issues include myriad concerns and human experiences, as well as many layers of social, political, and global context. Christianity in the United States, however, remains both fixated and polarized around the matter of the morality of homosexuality.[1] I resonated with Michael's point of view, and with his frustration, as well. The question itself pushes us toward polarized responses, and the focus of the question is extremely limited. I also sympathized with Ian, both in his well-intended attempt to phrase a question carefully, and in his sense that there are high stakes for everyone involved.

The limits of such narrow focus are reflected in conundrums that come up in religious settings, challenges that are growing more intense and frequent. A devout gay family joins a conservative church. Will the church recognize the validity of their family, or counsel the parents to live together in permanent celibacy, or to divorce? An employee at a Christian organization goes public as transgender, and their gender status is interpreted as a deviant sexual choice. Federal mandates for LGBTQ civil rights are interpreted in opposite ways by various Christian organizations, as necessary pushes toward social justice or as unjust intrusions against religious liberty. A male student once said to me, with no irony or sarcasm, "The college rules against homosexuality don't apply to me; I'm bisexual." A female student pondered, "It's all so sexual, and that's not what I'm questioning. I wonder how emotionally close I can get to my best friend before it starts, well, causing jealousy, and preventing me from even caring whether or not I date a guy."

1. For discussion of this polarization, see Brownson, *Bible, Gender, Sexuality*; Gritter, *Generous Spaciousness*; Gushee, *Changing Our Mind*; Vines, *God and the Gay Christian*.

Christian focus on homosexuality doesn't begin to address issues of bisexuality, lesbianism, transgender, transsexuality, gender bending, sexual fluidity, intersex, and all things queer, nor gender realities such as gender-based inequality and violence on a global level, and the roles of men and women in home, church, and society. The personal and moral focus of Christian concern does not address the need for a paradigm of political engagement by Christians in a pluralist society. Furthermore, I find it surprising when some Christians say, "Why are we constantly talking about homosexuality?" while, at the same time, others say, "We've got to start talking about homosexuality!" It seems there is too much talk, and too little, at the same time.

Michael speaks for many Christians today, frustrated with the question. Frustrated with how the issues are framed. Frustrated that it is even framed as an issue. Wanting to talk about things in a new way, with new conversation partners, and for new purposes. If Michael had raised his concern in my mostly-conservative-Christian class fifteen years ago, his classmates might have assumed he was liberal, evading the question and trying to make matters so ambiguous that we will all just slip right down the liberal slope with him. Today, even moral traditionalists often agree that "us-them" framings are unhelpful, that we must be on guard against discrimination, and that we probably need to rethink everything.

Rethinking the whole thing involves stepping back to examine nearly every word of the opening question, *how should we respond to homosexuals in the church*? Who is the *we* who responds, and what is it we should be doing? And who or what is it that we are engaging: persons, issues, policies, theologies, or something else? Is *homosexual* the proper word, and who determines the propriety of words and concepts? Why the focus on *we* and *our* church: what about our society, and the global community of all humans?

FINDING COURAGE TO LEAD DURING CONFLICT

Several years have passed since that class with Michael and Ian, but these lectures are devoted to probing their exchange. Chapter

1, "Beginning," recommends drawing a broader frame around the sex/gender complex, seeing the issues as interrelated, and all persons as both implicated and invited. The beginning, then, is an end to scapegoating, which is to heap the problems of the many onto the backs of a few. Chapter 2, "Conflicting," explores metaphors for sex/gender conflicts, offering a conflict transformation perspective. It outlines major social and religious changes that serve as both context and trigger for conflict, and shows how respecting the intensity and the dynamics of conflict is integral to working toward its transformation. Chapter 3, "Leading," draws all people toward courageous leadership, living with awareness of how sex/gender conflicts impact society and church, and taking wise action in one's own sphere of influence.

In sum, sex/gender issues are conflicts, ones that we are likely to live with for some time. Courageous leadership involves engaging conflict productively, even taking it up as a generative practice of Christian discipleship. This is not just for organizational leaders; rather, it is a call to all Christians to lead within their spheres of influence, including their own families and personal lives.

TAKE YOUR POSITIONS

At the end of my lectures, it is not uncommon for a listener or reader to reply, "But you never really got down to business! You never told us what you believe about homosexuality." This is, truly, what I believe about homosexuality: that it is part of a larger complex of issues that are best viewed and treated as conflict. My deepest belief is that believers must work together to engage productively in conflict, and that at the heart of this work is robust worship and Christian practice.

This answer is not satisfying, of course, and may even seem evasive. Such is the strength of the polarizing question, "Does the Bible say homosexuality is a sin?" It is a "bully question," shoving and pushing us to meet its demands. Whether "yes" or "no," the answer reveals much about the speaker: her view of Scripture, her view of morality, her politics, and her central or marginal belonging to some Christian tradition. It doesn't reveal much, however, about how to proceed in our challenging context with any hope for Christian unity, or even a lesser goal, a future with less division, despair, and brokenness.

If I must answer a question I haven't asked, and choose among answers that all seem less than satisfying, I'd answer in this way: I affirm the living, true, spiritual quality of Scripture, and that all of Scripture speaks to all of us. There are not a handful of verses about homosexuality; rather, there are tens of thousands of verses, each of which apply to every person. I believe every human life is created good and blessed, and that every life harbors brokenness and evil. In sexuality and gender as in the rest of life, the path leads to wholeness and integration, a remembering or reclamation of a created, blessed, wholeness of self and a full, satisfying connection with our Creator.

I believe in the *imago Dei*, individual conscience, and spiritual freedom, which leads me to an argument that abolitionists made, one that sits deep within the Baptist tradition of my ancestors. People must be free so they may freely choose Christ. Thus, I support institutional policies and theologies that create accountabilities for human evil and brokenness, but that honor individual conscience and protect space for people to freely choose holiness or sin, to freely repent, and thus to freely find Christ. In keeping with freedom, I support social justice and civil rights that recognize the place each citizen has in our polity.

I am persuaded by the many sincere LGBTQ believers who find in their conscience a requirement for celibacy, and by those who find freedom for sexual partnership and marriage. I honor and respect both. I don't find that my own view trumps the value of the diverse ways that sexual and gender minorities are fitting together their sexualities and their spiritualities. My anthropologist's eye is fascinated by the diversity of human experiences and by the speed and nature of social changes, and I am doing my best to pay close attention. Compassion, mercy, and wonder are the spiritual fruits ripening in me over these issues, not moral certainty (which, I'm pretty sure, isn't a spiritual fruit).

I hesitate to share these views not because I'm uncertain, but because the bully question reduces complexity to a binary. It ends conversation as it is just beginning. People walk out of a lecture or click away from a podcast or video as soon as they realize they disagree with the speaker about one key point of theology. It's a shame, because we're in this together, as Christians. We liberal, conservative, progressive, and post-whatever Christians. We complementarians and egalitarians. We Republicans and Democrats. We Methodists, Catholics, Pentecostals, non-denominationals, and so on. I want us to hang together and figure out how to remain in generative, loving relationship during this long, protracted conflict.

I have no hope whatsoever that everyone will agree on the moral question, or on the question of biblical authority, or on any political or institutional move. I do have hope for a deeper kind of unity, grounded in our love of God and neighbor, and nothing more than that. And I have hope that the many voices speaking on these issues will matter, each in their own way: personal stories from LGBTQ people and their loved ones, theological and exegetical work done by scholars, sermons preached by pastors, aspirational visions cast by musicians and artists, and questions of faith, society, and Christian living explored by teachers such as myself.

1

BEGINNING

I have been teaching Intro to Anthropology nearly every semester for fifteen years, and I begin each one with a reflection on Romans 12:1–2. This Scripture invites us to take up Paul's charge to the church at Rome, to take it up in our own time and place. Having laid a framework for reconciliation within the Roman church, Paul describes how believers should live their new life in Christ with each other, and with respect to society and external authorities. Likely in contrast to other forms of worship that downplayed rationality in favor of ecstasy, Paul encourages a right use of the mind.[1]

> Therefore, I urge you, brothers and sisters, in view of God's mercy, to offer your bodies as a living sacrifice, holy and pleasing to God—this is your true and proper worship. Do not conform to the pattern of this world, but be transformed by the renewing of your mind. Then you will be able to test and approve what God's will is—his good, pleasing and perfect will.[2]

1. Bray and Oden, *Romans;* Keener, *IVP Bible Background*, 438.
2. Rom 12:1–2, NIV.

We present our bodies—our lives, all that we've got—as ongoing, active and living sacrifices. That includes our brains, our talking, studying, and thinking, but also our hearts, our souls, and our daily lives.

We do all of this in the light of God's mercy. That means it's OK to get it wrong, to accidentally offend, to get angry and purposely offend, to change our minds, to expose deeper problems, or mistakenly create new ones. There's enough mercy for that.

My hope is that insights from anthropology will contribute to this effort in cross-disciplinary integration like an infusion, offering a little something helpful in many different areas. Anthropology is a broad discipline: Margaret Mead once said, "The world is my field; it's all anthropology."[3] Anthropologists are interested in the patterns of human life. Our epistemological gold standard is *being there*. Through ethnographic fieldwork, we come to know other ways of life by putting ourselves in the shoes of a cultural Other. For example, I learned how sexuality and spirituality influence inner-city neighborhood dynamics by doing fieldwork at a Metropolitan Community Church built in an inner-city neighborhood. The church encouraged members to relocate to the neighborhood and to shape a religiously centered gay urban area.[4] I worshiped at the church. I lived in the neighborhood. I talked with people in their homes, and experienced daily life in the neighborhood. Through immersion, anthropologists gain a rich, textured, compassionate perspective on the diversity of human life.

Anthropologists don't become the Other; rather, we straddle the roles of insider and outsider, as much as possible, coming away with a rich description of the pattern of life of a cultural Other, and a sense of how the Other makes meaning of life. In this way, anthropology's approach displays both the rigor of a science and the persuasive beauty of art. As anthropologist Eric Wolf describes, "Anthropology is both the most scientific of the humanities and the most humanistic of the sciences."[5] With rigorous method and

3. Sargeant, "It's All Anthropology."

4. Paris and Anderson, "Faith-based Queer Space."

5. American Anthropological Association, "This is Anthropology."

theory, anthropology yields compassion born of deep experience and understanding of the breadth of human ways of life.

The culture concept illuminates the "pattern of this world," including how humans adapt and adjust to different contexts, make meaning of life, and share those meanings and lifeways with others. Anthropologists describe and compare patterns in human ways of life that, on first glance, seem unrecognizable or even chaotic.[6] Sex, gender, and sexuality are three such patterns that are expressed with great variety across cultures. These domains of life are integral for family, reproduction, and socialization of the young. Thus, humans everywhere give close attention to sex, gender, and sexuality, developing an astonishingly broad range of cultural norms, as well as responses to, and life pathways for, those who breach norms.

Understanding patterns is an essential part of discernment and right action: we need to understand deeply that to which we are conforming, resisting, transforming, or rejecting.[7] Romans 12 is often read simplistically, as though believers ought to separate themselves from culture, or perhaps even conform society to the pattern of religious life. Such approaches stem from a misunderstanding of what it means to be human, and a misunderstanding of the rich, deep, and unavoidable interplay between religion and society. To be a-cultural, apart from culture, is to be non-human. Just as it wasn't good for Adam to be alone, it isn't possible for a human to come into being, nor to survive for even a few hours in infancy, without intensive relationship with other humans. Our sociality is part of the brilliance of our species, an expression of the *imago Dei*. Even the most separatist Christians—seventeenth-century Anabaptists, for example, or the Desert Fathers and Mothers—used culturally comprehensible vocabulary, body language, and foodways. They were thoroughly enculturated beings, even while separate in many significant ways. When reduced to a slogan, "Do Not Conform" lifts three words out of context, occluding

6. Hiebert, *Gospel in Human Contexts*; Howell and Paris, *Introducing Cultural Anthropology*.

7. Niebuhr, *Christ and Culture*.

3

the fullness of Paul's charge to worship, be transformed, and work together to discern how to live well in whatever cultural context we happen to find ourselves.

Cultivating deeper understanding may be assisted by study of anthropology or other scholarly disciplines, but study alone narrows the field too much toward rationality and intellect. Worship, rendering homage and reverence to God, is one of our richest resources for putting Paul's admonition into practice. Worship includes formal church services, but also service, solitude, nature, music, and prayer. Even further, as Brother Lawrence describes in *The Practice of the Presence of God*, all of life can become worship, including doing the dishes, cleaning the house, going to work, and caring for loved ones. Life becomes worship when we do anything and everything with attention to the presence of God in every moment.[8] Brother Lawrence describes it thus:

> The time of business does not with me differ from the time of prayer, and in the noise and clatter of my kitchen, while several persons are at the same time calling for different things, I possess God as in great tranquility as if I were upon my knees at the blessed sacrament.[9]

Anabaptists might call it Christian practice. Wesleyans might call it holy living. Various Christian traditions have different ways of describing this whole-life, sacrificial, and active leaning toward the sacred, what Paul calls worship. Worship is a beautiful form of attention, helping us learn to focus on what is important for long periods of time and return to the practice over and over again.[10] It is not our thinking, nor our debating, nor our voting, that will yield holiness. Rather, as we make our whole lives living sacrifices, our minds are transformed so we may discern what the will of God is, what is good and acceptable and perfect.

Worship and other Christian practices, of course, have not resulted in widespread agreement among Christians regarding

8. Lawrence, *Practice*.

9. Ibid., 12.

10. Dawn, *A Royal Waste of Time*; Smith, *Desiring the Kingdom*; Smith, *Imagining the Kingdom*.

our view of God's will concerning gender roles, gay ordination, gay marriage, or same-sex sexual ethics. Or abortion. Or divorce. Or proper treatment of women. Remarkable, how many of the church's trouble spots are about sex and gender. Remarkable, how consensus eludes us. When people defend or describe their positions, they often point out the obviousness of their view and the clarity of Scripture regarding it. Yet for many of these topics, entire books are devoted to describing diverse Christian views and the divergent theologies and exegeses that support them: *New Feminist Christianity: Many Voices, Many Views*, or *Two Views on Women in Ministry*.[11]

It's just not so simple, and that's a good thing. If it were, we'd use prayer or worship or Bible study as magic, a ritual guaranteed to produce results. Hermione from *Harry Potter* might call it the Religio Charm. Instead, we're offered faith; a living, trusting connection to the sacred filled with both clarity and mystery.

Many individuals have clarity of conscience about some or all of these issues, but as a church, a religious collective, we don't. Looking ahead, we likely won't, and this seems inevitable in a pluralist democracy where individuals are socialized for freedom of thought. My reflections are not intended to produce or even encourage homogenous theology or ethics regarding the leading sex/gender issues of our day. In fact, I don't think we need homogenous understandings, practices, or policies, in order to proceed discerningly toward what is good and acceptable and perfect.

We will "go meta," taking an aerial view of sex/gender conflicts that are often all-consuming at the local and personal level. I invite us to find the forest for the trees, to step back to evaluate who we are, what we're doing, and what is the nature of the issues we engage. Interdisciplinary dialogue is vital in this task, drawing together insights, concepts, and theories from anthropology, psychology, and theology. Such reflections can lift us out of the

11. Beck, et al., *Two Views;* Hunt and Neu, *New Feminist Christianity.* For discussion of how diverse views stem from a presumably perspicuous sacred text, see Smith, *Bible Made Impossible.*

immediacy of our local context so we can gather new wisdom and relationships and questions and ideas to take back to our daily work.

START WHERE YOU ARE

Some of you are probably new to these issues, and are, very literally, beginning. Others have worked on gender and sexuality issues for many years, but we too, are beginning anew each day. I encourage us all to consider ourselves beginners, a stance that welcomes learning and forms of practice that anticipate mistakes, change over time, and always-growing maturity. Let's be teachable, especially we who are teachers.

I began, and begin, as a lay person, an anthropologist, a woman, a wife and mother, and a United States citizen. I call myself heterosexual when the need arises, but mostly I live without a sexual identity label. As I'll explain in further detail later, at this point in life my sexuality is shaped mostly by my femaleness, and by the religious vow of marriage. While desire is important, I work on focusing it toward one man, as marriage requires of me, not toward men in general, as heterosexuality expects. I also find more in common with all women—in the life course of a female body and spirit—than with heterosexuals of all sexes. I was raised "fundagelical," deeply internalizing the values of obedience and authority, male dominance, and the legalism of fundamentalism, and also evangelical elements such as the justice impulse, Christian music and material culture, and an emphasis on education. I have always attended church, across various traditions: the Evangelical Covenant Church, Church of God (Anderson, IN), Mennonite Church USA, Brethren in Christ, and now the United Methodist Church.

My interest in gender and sexuality is anything but purely academic. I live the issues in many of my important social roles. Beginning with acknowledgment of one's own social location is vital in appreciating different Christian viewpoints and visions.

As a Christian college professor, I talk to students regularly about their romantic relationships, emerging sense of sexuality, and how it all connects with their faith.

As an anthropologist, I maintain professional standing in a field that actively promotes full equality for LGBTQ persons and all other persons.

As a child, I was raised in a church where the pastor molested boys. As a mother, I work hard to keep my three boys sexually safe at church, and I advocate for prevention and response in the church more broadly.

As a girl, I was taught to submit to men, but as a woman, I don't.

As a friend, I treasure my mutually supportive ties to people of various sexualities, and people with a variety of views about gender equality and sexuality.

As a citizen, I vote on issues that impact people far beyond the bounds of my religious community.

As a Christian, I live, worship, write, and speak in the midst of difference. With respect to same-sex sexuality, Christians around me affirm, negate, and resist moral and political binaries. They are engaged, disengaged, aware, unaware, too cool to care, and too convicted to converse.

It may seem that "Christian" could, or even should, serve as a master status that settles disputes between the values and demands of these various social roles, but it doesn't seem to do that in any simple way. While religious identity is very powerful, it can also be misused as a trump card that diminishes the importance of power dynamics and personal developmental processes, working against the humanizing and liberating capacity of religion. For example, same-sex attracted believers are often told to be "Christian" instead of "gay," because identity in Christ should trump all other identities. This may help the person delay growth in their sexual development, or repress sexuality for a longer period of time, but religious identity doesn't resolve the challenges of sexual identity; they are different, though related, elements of human life that both deserve space in a person's identity and life. Similarly, women who are treated with inequality in the church, or even physically abused at home, may be told to prioritize Christian identity over gender, forgoing a pursuit of justice or even bodily safety in favor of a compliant religiosity.

Religion doesn't need to dominate other parts of life in order to express its profound power; in fact, expressions of power that repress, silence, subjugate, and overrule are evil distortions of true religion on both corporate and personal levels. Instead of a trump card, Jesus offers the metaphor of salt, or light, the Gospel as a sort of infusion that influences all of life. When we present ourselves to God as living sacrifices, we come to these challenging issues not just with our minds, our theology, and our moral reasoning, but with our lives, including all dimensions of who we are in society. We can expect something of the sacred to manifest in our work, politics, family, friendships, and all other elements of our lives in the world. Additionally, our personal spiritual practices, corporate worship and ritual, service, and our quotidian tasks in all of our social roles, all matter. We can expect our personal faith, and our corporate religious allegiances, as well, to assert the influence of salt or light, not the power of a hammer or a megaphone.

TENDING THE TANGLES

This summer, I spent three months cutting a decade's growth of honeysuckle vines off a fence in my back yard. Honeysuckle is pretty and it smells sweet, but it is also an invasive plant that can take down trees and fences. My husband admired my tenacity, and I replied, "But such reward. It's a world of metaphors out here!" Untended things get entangled. It's hard work to get to the root of things. The wheat and the tares grow up together. Good things strain toward the light, despite obstacles.

In religious ritual, in yard work, in everyday life, and even in conflict, we do what we do in the light of God's mercy. We can expect the sacred to appear, though we can't anticipate when or how. But we can expect it, and name it when we see it. As Jesus said, "The wind blows wherever it pleases. You hear its sound, but you cannot tell where it comes from or where it is going. So it is with everyone born of the Spirit."[12]

With respect to conflict over sexuality, we may wish to see God in consensus, the church holding high the standard and being a light to which others are drawn. In fact, we see the opposite: diverse personal ethics, and church policies and practices that are contested and sometimes rapidly changing.

Even worse, we see church corruption, abuses of power, and sexual abuse. The tangles thicken, the choking intensifies. As organizations, church structures often mirror corporate structures, by legal and social necessity, in their power structures, finances, and legal dimensions. They suffer, then, from the same tendencies as non-religious corporations in misdirecting and wrongly consolidating power and resources. Religious leadership increasingly mimics secular celebrity, with great attention and acclaim granted to the few, while the many labor in obscurity. Celebrity leadership is highly public, mostly male, and plays on a national or international stage. It requires constant media presence, intense attention to one's own image and appearance, rapid production of saleable products, and gimmickry. This seems to support and encourage moral failing, narcissism, and utter corruption.

Church corruption and disorganization of power profoundly undercuts Christian leadership, not just in reputation, but in actuality. It diminishes credibility for all churches and pastors, not just the offending ones. Even if we could manage to overlook narcissism, celebrity, gimmickry and salesmanship, and even mistreatment of women and men, the widespread mistreatment of children in both Protestant and Catholic churches must give pause. Really, can we Christians really have anything to say at all, on any subject whatsoever, if we can't even prevent or adequately respond to sexual predation in our midst? That's a sexual issue, too, and critics are right to call us hypocrites if we look only at the speck in others' eyes, and not at the log in our own.

Even if we don't get it together with consensus, even if we fail miserably in our attempts to organize and corporatize the

12. John 3:8, NIV.

Christian life, and even if we make the tangles worse, still even then, the sacred appears. Sheer mercy it is; sheer grace.

There is a time for lament, and a time for repentance, and these times are sacred. There is a time for love, for joy, for peace and patience. A time for generosity, gentleness, and self-control. These are the fruits by which we recognize the Spirit among us. They appear regardless of our success or failure, in the midst of harmony or conflict or even self-inflicted disaster. After listing the fruits of the Spirit, Paul concludes, "Against these things there is no law."[13] These words seem especially poignant in this time of conflict and pressure regarding religious freedom in arenas including contraception, homosexuality, and transgender. Law is certainly important, but it is helpful to remember that no legal or social context will prevent us from expressing true spiritual fruit: peace, patience, kindness, gentleness, and self-control.

We so often begin talking about homosexuality by considering whether or not *they*, or *it*, is a sin in God's eyes, or in the biblical text. These are worthy questions, but better to start with the log in our own eye. Part of the pattern of this world is that Christians, and Christian churches, are hated because of mistreatment of LGBTQ persons. And divorced people. And women who have abortions. And women in general. And victims of religious abuse. We need to own that, not minimize or deflect it, and proceed accordingly.

We start by presenting our bodies to God, and this is our collective body. We start where we are. The light we follow is not that of our own righteousness; rather, it is God's mercy that lights our way.

THE "WE" WHO RESPONDS

When I assigned topics in that gender studies class (the one I mentioned in the Introduction), I offered students just a few words, like "parenting" or "workplace issues," and gave them the task of

13. Gal 5:23, NIV.

framing the issue with an appropriate question. When it came to Ian's group, I wasn't sure what to write: "homosexuality," "sexual minorities," or "LGBTQ." And what would they be discussing: morality, politics, persons, issues, experiences, or statistics? I just wrote "LGBTQ," and let them run with it, which sufficed for an hour in class. But in life, the questions we ask matter very much.

"How should *we* respond to homosexuals in the church?" Again, who is the *we* that engages these matters, and what are *we* trying to accomplish? Are we solving a problem, addressing a need, helping the hurting, or respecting the dignity of a minority group? Is our posture one of engaging, listening, telling, responding, reacting, shaping, teaching, or defending? How would we recognize success: would the issues go away, be integrated, avoided, healed, respected, or celebrated? Would we have agreement, or agree to disagree? Is the heart of the issue focused on persons, politics, issues, theological ideas, moral boundaries, and is it local, national, or global?

All these balls are in the air at once, of course, and both traditionalist and progressive Christians often run into problems when we resort to our default approach. Even when we know it is no longer the case, traditionalists often ask questions and engage matters as if *we* are heterosexual, and theologically homogeneous within a church or Christian gathering. Traditionalists often prioritize the question of sexual morality at the level of the individual, and make other topics and matters defer to that priority. Progressives often do the same, but with a priority on social justice.

Simply, our sense of *we* needs to be accurate. We are the people of God. We are the people who pray, read, and tell stories in the line of Abraham and Sarah, of David, of Mary and Joseph, and of Jesus. We are witnesses of what we've seen and heard of the sacred. We are called to bear the light burden and the easy yoke of Jesus' law, which is love.

Yet to make a generalization about, well, every single Christian church or college or seminary I've been to in recent years, every group of two or more Christians I've come across, *we* don't all agree. We aren't all straight. We don't read the Bible in the same way. We don't vote, think, or see morality the same way. We are not all conservative, or liberal, or progressive, or post-whatever.

Many Christians are beyond ready to move past framing the issues in us-them, we-they terms—terms that "otherize" the Other and leave the self an unmarked category. What we move toward, then, is a bigger table with more chairs set at it. We people, all people of the earth. We the people of God. We, whoever is at a particular gathering, with each person included in the whole.

The "buts" speak up quickly. But what about a unified moral stance? But what about the sanctity of marriage? But what about leadership in the church? But what about teaching our children properly? It's not that these things have no importance, but a re-framing of the *we*, a frame that includes disagreeing voices as equal participants, de-centers these "buts" in favor of a more important core. This is not mere inclusion or even respect; rather, it is a con-sequential theological shift. If we honor the church as it is—that is, consisting of those who self-identify as Christians and wish to be part of the Christian movement—then we move forward together, with whoever chooses to be a part. This is different, theologically and ecclesiologically, than screening the church, or a given church, for acceptable members, and moving forward with only the "true believers."

A broader "we" doesn't offer moral affirmation to everyone, nor does it acknowledge the true faith or salvation of every person. On the other hand, it also doesn't create tiers of members, all of whom are invited to belong, but only some of whom are top-tier. This is the most welcoming form of traditionalism, "accepting but not approving," being kind and friendly to all, but reserving leadership, decision-making, stage time, and marriage, only for some. A broader "we" allows the wheat and the tares to grow up together, leaving judgment to God. This still requires discernment, and at times, exclusion from leadership or perhaps even exclusion from the community. Such discernment should happen on a much more nuanced basis than categorical inclusion or exclusion based on sexual feelings, or on one's moral stance regarding expression of those sexual feelings. A more robust communal process of discernment might rely on church tradition and history, the living witness of believers around the world, close relationship with others in our immediate context, Scripture, common sense and reason, and the living movement of the Holy Spirit among us. This requires complex, committed, ongoing conversation and work, ideally grounded in friendship and worship at the local level.

Homosexuality is a trigger issue not simply because it's about sex; it drives us quickly to consider who we are as the body of Christ: who belongs and who doesn't, and who gets to decide. It takes us deep into questions of faith and life: how should we live, and how will we know, and where are our guides for knowledge and for holiness? We have age-old resources for answering these questions, of course, but in two thousand years of Christian history, the questions have not been answered once and for all. With the cloud of witnesses from the past, we ask them anew, in a new context and with new social realities such as same-sex marriage, transgender, and LGBTQ church leadership. These questions are urgent, poignant, and simultaneously intimate and personal, and political and public.

RESPONDING TO "THEM"

We must address an even more challenging question: who are *they* to whom we respond? A poster at a religious institution announced an event devoted to "listening to LGBTQ voices." A member of the institution protested not the event, which he said was worthwhile, but the language on the poster. "LGBTQ," he said, was a "word with an agenda." Honoring the self-identification of sexual minorities was, in his view, a step toward the slippery slope of moral relativism. He recommended the word "homosexual," because it carries connotations of medical deviance and sin, connotations that must be retained. "We can talk about any subject here," he explained, "but we should be in charge of how it is named and framed."

Indeed, names are consequential. As anthropologist Clifford Geertz wrote, "Man is an animal suspended in webs of significance he himself has spun."[14] Names, labels, and categories are vitally important elements of human culture, shared ways of interpreting and living in the world. Physicist Varadaraja Raman, a Hindu, meditates each morning on symbols of numbers, music, and science, describing this as an aesthetic experience. "I'm well aware that ultimately all these are symbols and that they may not reflect exactly what is out there. But we live in symbols as long as we are cultural beings. . ."[15]

Genesis 2:19–20 describes God giving humans responsibility for naming creation.

> Now the LORD God had formed out of the ground all the beasts of the field and all the birds of the air. He brought them to the man to see what he would name them; and whatever the man called each living creature, that was its name. So the man gave names to all the livestock, the birds of the air and all the beasts of the field.[16]

Names create realities: consider the consequences of calling someone worthless, ugly, and stupid, or worthy, loved, and smart. If a smart boy perceives himself as stupid, his perception creates a consequential reality. Our words and understandings cannot be perfect representations of God's creational intent; God gave humans the responsibility to create these understandings from a subject position of humanity, a position with inherent benefits and limitations. It's hard enough to name elements of nature; asking about the status of a tomato (fruit or vegetable?) can spark a dinner party's worth of debate. Understanding humanity is even more challenging, and the stakes are very high. Europeans labeled Africans as closer to apes than to humans. Medical professionals have miscategorized female ambition and emotion as hysteria. Same-sex attraction has been coded as mental illness. Humans make sense of God's creation; making culture is part of the creation mandate

---

14. Geertz, *Interpretation of Cultures*.

15. Raman, "Heart's Reason," 134.

16. Gen 2:19–20, NIV.

to be stewards of creation. We live with the consequences of our naming, for good and for ill.

How do we name same-sex sexuality? What do we call it, what does it mean, and how does it fit in society and in individual identities and life narratives? Within the church, do we wish to follow society's patterns of naming and understanding sexuality, or develop alternate understandings, and what are the benefits and challenges in the direction we choose?

Christian engagement with sex/gender realities is mostly derived from the ways in which the issues are framed in society. This is often noted as a criticism: Christians creating knock-off ideas and artifacts just shortly after they've become passé elsewhere. It isn't intended as criticism, however. Religion and society exist in relationship of mutual influence. When religion is politically and culturally dominant, it appears as a guardian, or steward, of culture. Colonial America's sodomy laws, for example, are as Christian as they are American. When its worldly power diminishes, religion shifts to a responsive position. This demonstrates the powerful adaptive capacity of religion. We can expect to see it, in various social contexts, as dominant, marginal, responsive, public, privatized, and so on.

Christians have developed views of same-sex sexuality that have been linked to, or are derivative of, the philosophies and paradigms of the broader society. In the West, same-sex sexuality has been viewed and named in a variety of ways. The word "homosexuality" has been used only since the late nineteenth century, and even that has taken a variety of definitions and connotations. By the mid-nineteenth century, the notion of a "sexual instinct" was explored by writers and scientists, with various labels offered, such as heterogenit, monosexual, Dioning, and Urning. "Heterosexual," for a time, referred to abnormal sex between a man and a woman—that is, nonprocreative sex. Heterosexuality as we know it, focused mostly on sexual desire, and detached from genital expression (a virgin can be a heterosexual) and procreative intent, is a later version of the concept.[17]

17. Blank, *Straight;* D'Emilio and Freedman, *Intimate Matters;* Foucault,

Same-sex sexuality has been seen as a volitional sin, a behavior akin to lying or stealing. This formulation emerged from a moment of strong confluence between religion and mainstream society. In this view, the homosexual should choose to stop doing the offensive act.

It has been seen as a crime, the crime of sodomy. This is the strongest institutionalization of the separation of identity from behavior, criminalizing only the behavior. Similar to volitional sin, this view encourages the sodomite to stop performing certain behaviors.

Same-sex sexuality has been seen as a mental illness, an expression of a brain or psychological condition. Accordingly, the homosexual may seek medication, lobotomy, castration, aversion therapy, or other forms of psychological intervention that would restore the brain to the normal and healthy state of opposite-sex desire.

It has been seen as a sickness or addiction, similar to alcoholism. In this view, the homosexual may move toward restored health through twelve-step support programs or by white-knuckling it to sobriety (meaning either celibacy or heterosexuality).

On the affirming side, same-sex sexuality has been seen as a blessing, or as a creation of God. In this view, it should not simply be accepted, but celebrated and appreciated.

Same-sex sexuality has also existed as an unspeakable element of some people's experience, the "love that dare not speak its name."

Sociologist Stephen O. Murray catalogued ethnographic evidence about same-sex sexuality.[18] He asked, is homosexuality cross-culturally normative, or even universal? If it is, this would provide strong rationale for diminishing social stigma in our society. His research inquiry was designed to support socially progressive change, so the answer is even more surprising. Murray

---

History of Sexuality; Irvine, *Disorders of Desire.*

18. Murray, *Homosexualities.* See also Greenberg, *Construction of Homosexuality;* Wiesner-Hanks, *Gender in History.*

concluded that while same-sex sexuality is very common, homo-sexuality is rare.

Murray's *Homosexualities* was published in 2000, and today, the frame would more likely be LGB (highlighting different sexu-alities), or LGBTQ+ (including sexualities, gender, and all who wish to include themselves with categories of "queer" or "plus"), or simply "gay" (the most parsimonious way of including differ-ent sexualities). Available ethnographic evidence is almost entirely about male-male relations, and while he makes great effort to in-clude female-female relations, there simply isn't as much evidence, due either to female-female relations being less frequent, or due to male bias in ethnographic fieldwork. Data on bisexuality is even scarcer, and his book doesn't attempt to translate "trans" or "queer" or other newer labels from our society across ethnographic cases. For this reason, I use the word "homosexuality" as he did, even while acknowledging that in our society, labels and sexual expres-sions have diversified.

Homosexuality is one of four patterns, or cultural configura-tions, of same-sex intimacies. Homosexuality is a predominantly modern form of same-sex relations that involves relative social equals in romantic, intimate relations that may be life-long, and now, may include legal marriage. It is a social role and personal identity that correlates with inner feelings or orientation related to sexual partner choice.[19]

Murray sees homosexuality in pre-modern contexts includ-ing among Khoisan language speakers (southeastern Africa), and in Melanesian and Polynesian societies. In the best documented cases, however, these seem different than modern homosexuality in that they involve same-sex activity among young, unmarried lovers or friends, individuals who spend most of their adult lives in opposite-sex marriages that are typically procreative

Modern homosexuality is unique, then, in involving a group consciousness of sexual identity, subcultures that support the lives of sexual minorities, and relationships that have the possibility of being life-long, exclusive, and legally validated. It is a sensible

19. Murray, *Homosexualities,* 382.

cultural adaptation in modern contexts where individual rights are honored, the "sexual instinct" has been named and considered increasingly important in human identity, and in societies that are urban, pluralist, and large-scale enough to allow for the development of robust subcultures.

The second is age-graded same-sex relations, in which difference of age between partners is vital, most commonly a relationship between a man and a boy. This triggers distaste because such relations are seen as unethical and illegal in many modern societies. Christians will be familiar with age-graded same-sex relations from Roman practices in the New Testament period.[20] Same-sex intimacy was believed to masculinize boys, making them warriors and true men by distancing them from the household world of mothers and sisters, and immersing them in the world of men. Additionally, sex was seen as part of status, so a powerful Roman man could claim sexual access to any social inferior, women or men, girl or boy. This was not indicative of homosexuality or bisexuality; rather, voracious and expansive sexual appetite symbolized virile masculinity. In these relations, the notion of sexual orientation, or the centrality of desire, is not at play, different than our notion of homosexuality. It would be normal for a man or boy who engages in same-sex activity to also be sexually interested in women.

The third pattern is gender-differentiated same-sex relations. Here, the most important element is that the partners show differentiated gender displays. The mid-twentieth century lesbian butch-femme partnership is an example, one that many people offensively project onto modern lesbian, gay, and bisexual couples when they ask, "Who's the man? Who's the woman?" Today, most same-sex couples are defined by their sexual orientation and identity, not by gender display. The Samoan fa'afafine provide a different example, in which men dress and live as women, flamboyantly expressing feminine excess.[21]

20. Greenberg, *Construction*.
21. Nanda, *Gender Diversity*.

An earlier typology used a fourth category, profession-based same-sex relations.[22] Profession-based same-sex relations involve individuals who take part in same-sex relations as part of a job, usually prostitution, performance, or sacred roles. The hijras of India, natal men who are castrated and dress in feminine dress, live as a third gender, neither man nor woman.[23] Traditionally, hijras offered ritual blessings for those in traditional genders at key life transitions such as marriage and childbirth. The sexuality of the hijra was not considered central to their third gender role. Today, however, many hijra earn money in exchange for sexual acts. The notable feature of this category is that, contrary to the assumptions of modern homosexuality, same-sex relations may or may not stem from desire or identity; it can be just a job.

In Murray's estimation, the "modern homosexual," or what we might now label "lesbian, gay, or bisexual" is a new historical form, a pattern of this world that makes meaning of same-sex desire in a particular way. In short, same-sex desire is seen as linked to orientation, or to sexual identity, and when that identity is lived out in sexual partnership, it is a romantic partnership between relative social equals that may result in a life-long commitment that may or may not include legal marriage. It is a same-sex sexual and relational trajectory, or life script, that more or less parallels opposite-sex relationships.

CHRISTIAN RESPONSES TO CULTURAL PATTERNS

As the notion of sexual identity has become stronger since the mid-twentieth century—that is, the notion that the direction of one's sexual feelings constitutes a central part of one's social and personal identity—earlier constructions of homosexuality have fallen away in favor of a view of LGBTQ lives and identities as socially credible lifeways grounded in a sexual essence, or identity, that resides within each individual self, made known through

22. Murray argues that this category is best subsumed under gender-stratified same-sex relations.

23. Nanda, *Neither Man Nor Woman*.

desires. Whether sexualities, or sexual identities, exist by choice or by nature, and whether or not they are moral, are not central concerns. That they *are*, and that groups feel strongly about living out these identities as full and equal citizens, and that they do so without harming others in ways that violate laws, is sufficient for moving toward legal equality and social tolerance.

Should Christians, then, conform to this pattern of the world, or do something different? If our worship were to transform us and renew our minds, what would we think? What would we do? These are the questions when, as individuals and organizations, we need to decide whether or not to accept a person's self-iden-tification, or whether to comply with federal law, or whether to change our vocabulary as society's new words emerge. Answers are required, most often, in very specific cases: what to write on the poster, whether this particular person can serve in leadership, and so on. Keep in mind that we very often conform to the pattern of the world because Christianity is incarnational, existing within culture. For example, we speak English, use Power Point, and drive cars. All elements of culture shape us, even those that seem neutral or insignificant.

Christians sometimes keep alive earlier social notions, for example, that homosexuality is a volitional sin, a crime against God, an illness, a medical abnormality, or an addiction. Christian understandings derived from earlier mainstream cultural under-standings seem not only cruel and bizarre, but literally nonsen-sical: they simply don't make sense using contemporary thought paradigms. This is akin to missionaries who refuse to learn the local language, attempting to convey the Gospel with symbols and concepts that are not embedded in local understandings.

The necessity of being Christian in culture is reflected in the fact that we can even ask the question, "Does the Bible say homo-sexuality is a sin?" Human sexuality is certainly a strong concern in Scripture, from beginning to end, but the word *homosexual* didn't appear in Bibles until the late 1940s.[24] The Greek words *malakoi* and *arsenokoitai*, in 1 Corinthians 6:9–11, came into twentieth-

---

24. Ontario Consultants, "Homosexuality"; Slick, "Word 'Homosexual.'"

century English translations with a variety of terms: effeminate, homosexuals, male prostitutes, boy prostitutes, pederasts, perverts, sodomites, abusers of themselves with men, homosexual offenders, liers with mankind, passive homosexual partners, and "those who use and abuse sex" (this broadest translation from The Message).[25]

By necessity, study of Scripture is a cross-cultural task, most obviously apparent in the effort of translation. The word homosexual wasn't in Scripture earlier because it wasn't sufficiently present in the vocabularies of English-speaking Bible readers. The word appears in English lexicons in the late nineteenth century as a medical term, and definitions for both homosexuality and heterosexuality didn't stabilize until the early twentieth century. Translators understood the emergence of the notion of sexual identity, and words such as homosexual, or lesbian, and so on, and brought these new English words and concepts into English translations when they were widespread enough to have become the best available approximations for Hebrew and Greek terms. Clearly, understanding how Scripture speaks to us today is a cross-cultural challenge, even more so when detailed knowledge of a Greek word in its original context is limited or unavailable.

Translators' determinations are immensely important, for example, when listing forms of unrighteousness that would prevent a person from inheriting the kingdom of heaven. A different challenge comes from newly coined terms that cannot be correlated with biblical words, such as *heterosexual, lesbian, trans,* or *sexual identity.* Other culturally specific concepts about which we need moral determinations and guidance include *democracy, Internet,* and *teenager.* Approximations for those specific words do not exist in biblical languages, and so we must look to broader themes, narratives, and laws in Scripture that may apply, across great distance of time, space, and culture, to cultural forms not indigenous to original biblical contexts.

To say that sexual identity is a social construction is to say that we have responsibility for how we name things, a God-given

25. Ontario Consultants, "Homosexuality."

responsibility. Our words and names have consequence; they construct our reality. A frustrating conservative Christian appropriation of the notion of social construction is to conclude that if homosexuality is a social construction, then it is *merely* social, which is to say it is less than really real, perhaps even a delusion of the so-called homosexual. LGBTQ people correctly protest this appropriation, insisting that their identities, their personhood, their families, and their loves, are very much real.

Frustrating, too, is our tendency to focus only on the few. This is the temptation to scapegoat, heaping the sins of the many onto the backs of a few. We may bemoan divorce, without considering the deep challenges to all life partnerships, including marriage. We may focus on the "problem" of homosexuality, instead of at the opportunities and challenges in the full life cycle of sexuality for all humans. Gender issues are almost always focused on women, instead of at human beings, all of whom are gendered.

A real transformation involves not merely answering the dominating questions about what *we* think of *them*. Transformation invites a broader frame, fuller questions, and a more expansive invitation to discipleship. When we interrogate all categories, we implicate and invite all persons toward moral and theological reflection. Historian Jonathan Ned Katz probes the origins of heterosexuality, and describes its fascination.

> Unless pressed . . . we fail to name the "norm," the "normal," and the social process of "normalization," much less consider them perplexing, fit subjects for probing questions. Analysis of the "abnormal," the "deviant," the "different" and "other," "minority" cultures has seemingly held much greater charm. Yet the deep desire possessing some of us to dress in the clothes of our own sex, and the profound conviction of some of us that we feel like the sex we are—if we think about these emotions—are quite as puzzling and complex as transvestism and transsexualism. Why should external norms of dress and sex have such deep, powerful internal holds on so many of us?[26]

26. Katz, *Invention of Heterosexuality*, 16.

Katz describes heterosexuality as homosexuality's fraternal twin, siblings emerging together in the early twentieth century, depending on one another for existence. Heterosexuality serves many social purposes. It marks the norm against which others deviate. It is a category of privilege. It provides a frame for understanding personal identity and relationships. It organizes the field of potential sexual or marital mates.

Heterosexuality can be queried, just as homosexuality can be, and for more than its consequences for personal morality. These categories highlight an important part of human life—sexual desire, partnership, and social affiliation—but do they name it well? Personally, I find more in common with women, as a category, than with heterosexuals. I find heterosexual male sexual expressions, fantasies, and media to be Other. While women's sexual expressions are also broad and diverse, they seem more comprehensible to me. I also find the pressure of displaying conformity and loyalty to heterosexuality to be at odds with my Christian discipleship. Christian discipleship calls for honest, vulnerable repentance and restoration before God; that is, all of a person's sexuality and gender in all of its health and distress. Heterosexuality functions like a club to which one may belong by feeling, or at least claiming to feel, certain sexual feelings. That doesn't leave enough room for full development of a life, including a sexual journey, which by definition can't be known in advance, and which contains mystery and clarity, delight and humiliation, glory and shame. I want room for my true life and true self to unfold, and to be shaped and deeply known by God and by my loved ones, without club membership being always in question. Needless to say, Christianity can often function in this way as well, a club from which a member in good standing may fall due to certain thoughts, doubts, words, or behaviors. It is no surprise, then, that many Christian heterosexuals have such a hard time being honest about how sexuality and spirituality fit together in their lives.

In another sense, I share more in common with all other human beings than with any other species. It is important to hold humanity together and recognize our unity, even as we label and explore our differences. In this way, *they* are *we*, and what we are addressing are questions of human sexuality, not the issues of a small minority.

But even beyond this, let's reframe the issue so there is more within the frame. It is better viewed as the "sex-gender complex," a complex or compendium of issues that cluster around the sex-gender domain of life. The sex-gender complex includes healthy sexuality across the life course, as well as abortion, sex trafficking, divorce, premarital chastity, gender roles, women's work, childcare, gender and authority in church and society, sexual violence in the church, and power—and lesbian, gay, transgender, queer, transsexual, gender-bending, bisexual, heterosexual issues, and the myriad ways these intersect with race, ethnicity, and social class.

It's a complex complex, but this broad frame holds together more pieces, and more people, and more of our human experience. It is misguided to pick out one piece and attempt to understand it, or blame and isolate it, or try to do away with it. It all hangs together: what happens in one domain influences the others.

BEGINNING, IN LIGHT OF GOD'S MERCY

In conclusion, who are we, and what are we doing? When we begin, what are we beginning? We begin with flux, fluidity, and flow in our world, our language, our concepts, and even our own sexual lives. The pattern of this world shifts rapidly, making it difficult to pin down a response, or a mode of engagement. This may feel frustrating for Christians who conceptualize their faith with very fixed terms. It may be frustrating in a different way for those ready to move in a direction, not to keep rehashing the beginning.

This highlights the ongoing importance of the hermeneutical task, the cross-cultural work of connecting our lives to the story of God's people across time and across great cultural difference, and now, in a time of extremely rapid and deep social change. Our Scripture is a living text, and we know a living God, and so we adjust and adapt and learn and change, by necessity, but also hopefully with humor and grace.

Tim Otto offers helpful advice for we who take up these issues within religious settings. Tim is a gay Christian who has lived for many years in an intentional community in San Francisco. He defies simple liberal-conservative categories with his personal and religious life, though he engages them intelligently when necessary. In response to my question, "what are we doing?" he offers this:

> . . . rather than latching onto whether same-sex relationships are right or wrong, a better initial question might be: how is God working for the good? How is God working for the good through the controversy in the church around homosexuality? How is God working for the good through Christians who identify themselves as LGBTQ?[27]

He encourages us to reach and wrestle for

> . . . a truth bigger than "right or wrong" judgments, a truth that requires costly changes in how we live. . . . If Christians are going to make any kind of intelligible case one way or the other, we will need to form faith communities that demand far more of all Christians—communities that make us odd, generous blessings to the world.[28]

This circles back to church corruption, our deep collective failings. When we focus on moral certainty, we often wrestle more precision from the Bible than it offers regarding sexual behavior, replete as it is with stories in which polygamy, concubines, and arranged marriage flow without critique or commentary. Our persistent focus on the personal moral behaviors of LGBTQ people, a small percent of the population, leaves us open to the charge of looking for specks in other people's eyes, and even worse, makes us vulnerable to overlooking or mishandling egregious sexual abuse against children and women and men, and other expressions of misogyny.

27. Otto, *Oriented to Faith,* xvi.
28. Ibid., xix.

A different focus might hinge on how we live, the quality of our communities, our capacity to be generous in blessing: this is offering our bodies, personally, and our collective body, the church, as living sacrifices. It puts us in position to be transformed, though it is no technique or tool or charm for making that happen on our terms. Such a focus includes personal sexual morality, of course, for people of all sexual orientations, but it holds this vulnerable pursuit, one that easily triggers shame and humiliation, within a bigger, more loving and joyous, community life.

Our Christian traditions draw us into repetitive behaviors, rituals that influence how we live, think, know, and act. Transformation happens via the ordinary, repetitive elements of the Christian life: prayer, worship, service, family, friendship. We don't need to get it all right regarding sex and gender before we can pray, worship, and serve well. Rather, the fruits of our ordinary practice ripen and fall into our open hands as we approach deep, protracted conflict around sex/gender issues such as homosexuality, abortion, or roles of men and women.[29]

We begin with the ordinary, repetitive practices that shape us and mark us as the people of God. We begin by expecting the sacred, and naming it when we see it. We begin in a profoundly challenging context, from within a church that is, by necessity, organized according to the patterns of a globalized, modern, democratic society.

We begin from within a church that has failed, and continues to fail, to protect the well-being of the vulnerable.

We begin our work on same-sex sexuality when we haven't yet figured out to handle human sexuality.

We begin with flux and rapid change, and this is how things will likely remain, at least for the foreseeable future.

We can expect that our failures and our limitations will open us up to receive mercy, and to practice lament, and to work toward repentance, and that this work will be fruitful. The invitation is to step up to courageous leadership in Christian sex-gender conflicts. Let's go meta, and take an aerial view of conflicts that are so

29. MacIntyre, *After Virtue*.

consuming at the local level. Let's work together to discern God's will, moving forward together in and through conflict.

We won't be able to get it all right. We may use inadequate words and concepts. We may misunderstand. We may misspeak. We may not agree, not even within a church, not even within a family, maybe not even within our own minds.

But here's what we *can* do, and we can do it well. We can practice our faith. We can be teachable. We can live in light of God's mercy, and trust that this is the only hope we have of living well.

2

CONFLICTING

You see something in the distance, perhaps a man in what seems to be a blue leotard and cape, flying. You might wonder what it is. You might say, "It's a bird . . . it's a plane . . . it's Superman!"

You hear an explosive sound nearby. Could it be a car backfiring, or gunshots, or the neighbor kid's science project?

You hear the sound of your baby crying upstairs. Is he winding down or ramping up?

Discerning the nature of things is important because our actions stem from how we define situations, and how we perceive the motives and actions of others. Right action is rooted in—and fosters—love, compassion, gentleness, and self-control: the fruits of the spirit. While we can't control or predict outcomes, we can choose well-intended, well-considered action. What we do is part of our living sacrifice, offered in light of God's mercy.

This chapter asks, "It's a bird, it's a plane, it's a what?" with respect to how Christians engage the sex/gender complex as a whole, and it will focus on same-sex issues. We'll explore the dynamics of conflict and the challenges of rapid social change, and conclude by asking a lot of questions. I'll invite you to choose a few for yourself to take away.

CONFLICTS OVER SEX AND GENDER

At various times in United States history, Christians have viewed same-sex sexuality as a sin, a crime, a mental illness, a disease, an addiction, an unspeakable abnormality, or a normal variation within God's good creation. Making categories and languages is part of human creativity and responsibility, given by God, so we can expect to see change over time, and we can expect to see better or worse utility and accuracy at different times. Using Stephen Murray's anthropological approach, I concluded that modern homosexuality (already an outdated phrase) is a distinctive cultural form that frames same-sex relationships as parallel to opposite-sex relationships, ideally between relative social equals, with relational dynamics of friendship and intimacy and family.

Western societies are strengthening this cultural form with legal marriage, civil unions, and other forms of mainstream recognition. Religious responses vary, and these responses are sometimes crafted voluntarily and sometimes under legal mandate. In the United States, same-sex marriage is now legal in all states, and the Supreme Court explained their decision as a matter of honoring constitutional principles of justice, equality, and individual rights. Many US Christian church-goers, however, attend churches that refuse to endorse same-sex marriage, grounded in their views of Scripture. A smaller portion of US Christians attend churches within denominations where pastors are allowed to perform same-sex marriages (groups such as the Evangelical Lutheran Church in America, the Episcopal Church, the Presbyterian Church [USA], the United Church of Christ, and the Unitarian Universalist Association).[1]

The disjuncture between social change and religious norms is intensifying. Christian groups sometimes adapt to social change,

1. Priest, "Unpublished."

and sometimes resist, but there is no question that Christian traditionalists are in a defensive position. *Washington Post* columnist Michael Gerson reflects on how rapid social change is creating pressure for Christian colleges, including his alma mater Wheaton College, to change community codes of behavior.[2] He elucidates College Board David Coleman's concept of "patient pluralism," that is, that a pluralist society should not use intimidation and public humiliation to force conservatives toward progressive change. Patient pluralism would tolerate diverse views, giving time and space for conservatives to process the issues, and implement change, in a manner more organic to their values and organizations. This is a vastly different argument than an assertive, powerful one upholding a traditional biblical view of marriage and sexuality, explaining that this is also the common good for society. When religion was in a guardian position vis-à-vis society, such an assertive argument would be persuasive, and it was often made throughout the second half of the twentieth century. Now, the most that conservatives can ask for, it seems, is for society to tolerate their slow pace of change, but the eventual outcome seems already determined: change they must.

As if this weren't enough, it's not just sexual identity that we see flying through the sky. It seems like a different form, or perhaps the same form, but in clearer view. It's not same-sex sexuality, in and of itself; rather, it's the larger set of issues we keep trying to figure out within the church: abortion, divorce, contraception, premarital chastity, marriage, women working, daycare, pornography, addictions, child abuse, sex trafficking, teaching youth about sex and gender—and heterosexuality, lesbian, gay, bisexuality, trans, queer, intersex, asexuality, and gender-bending. All that, plus whatever is about to come up next. It's hard to miss, but it's also hard to see clearly.

In my work with churches and church-related colleges, and in my personal life as well, I hear many metaphors used to describe all of this. It's a problem to be solved. It's a challenge we face. It's a fire to put out. It's a train wreck that we can't avoid. It's an offense

2. Gerson, "An Appeal."

against God. It's disorder. It's unnatural. It's a gift. It's a blessing from God. It's an opportunity. It's natural. It's just not a big deal. It's the biggest deal.

Metaphors too easily foster wrong action. They encourage us to avoid or repress, hoping the fire flares up somewhere other than our church or school. They encourage us to fix the problem, but this "problem" includes people, and people generally don't appreciate it when you try to fix them. Additionally, while they may not encourage it, negative metaphors leave space for cruelty and meanness, carried out in God's name.

Positive metaphors, however, seem premature, or even distracting, such as when Christians distract a person from grief or crisis by recommending they count their blessings. These issues are not gifts in the same sense as, say, a bouquet of flowers. When I receive flowers, it immediately makes me happy and I say, "Thank you!" That isn't my response when Christians disagree about sex/gender issues. It usually elicits a stress response, heightened pulse, concern, and watchfulness.

Those encouraging a gift framework often put LGBTQ persons front and center. How can you argue against viewing a human person as a gift? The gift framework insists, "Persons are gifts! Don't you value persons? If you do, you'll agree with us." This framework is loaded: if you disagree, or believe homosexuality to be a sin, you are at the same time denigrating the value of a person. Such a loaded framework is simply a different spin on the traditionalist framework that insists, "The Bible is authoritative! Don't you value the Bible? If you do, you'll agree with us." In either case, those who disagree have crossed a serious line and find themselves on the wrong side of propriety, intelligence, belonging, or even salvation.

The challenge is to frame the issue in such a way as to keep everyone engaged, including traditionalists and progressives and those who don't fit either of those categories. People may opt out because they are too convicted to converse, too cool to care, or hateful in their separatism, but the framework itself should not serve as a tacit filter.

I recommend framing the sex/gender complex as a social conflict. This conflict extends far beyond homosexuality to all heterosexual and LGBTQ realities, gender norms for masculinity and femininity, as well as gender non-normativity, and negotiation of gender roles in general. I find it helpful to name it plainly, with a framework that honors both the danger and damage of conflict, and the potential for its transformation. When congregations split, families argue, individuals live in torment, struggling with suicide and self-harm, that is conflict. We may hope and pray that gifts emerge from it, but it is still conflict.

Throughout the *Harry Potter* series, characters refer to Lord Voldemort, the antagonist, as "You Know Who." Afraid to even utter his name, most characters avoid Voldemort and hope he won't return. The final action scene seems to be the climax of the narrative, but after the sparks and smoke and unicorn's blood have settled, a more important narrative turn occurs when Harry talks with his mentor, Dumbledore. Harry nearly utters Voldermort's name, but interrupts himself to substitute "You Know Who." Dumbledore corrects Harry, "Call him Voldemort, Harry. Always use the proper name for things. Fear of a name increases fear of the thing itself."[3]

Indeed, Harry's willingness—insistence, eventually—on using Voldemort's real name is one of the most important marks of Harry's leadership. His power derives not primarily from the lightning bolt on his forehead, his broomstick skills, or his cloak of invisibility. His power flows from his courage, seen in his willingness to name plainly that which makes others whisper.

When we name our situation clearly—that is, as a conflict— we gain power to engage it honestly and straightforwardly. While others avoid, deny, whitewash, or inflame the situation by naming it sideways or avoiding it altogether, true leadership will flow from people and organizations willing to plainly name what is happening. Of course, leadership and power do not always coincide, nor do truth and power. There is great power in avoidance, denial, and hatred. If Harry Potter teaches us anything, it is that true power

3. Rowling, *Harry Potter*, 298.

shines eventually and wins the day, and true hearts recognize it all along the way.

Instead of a train wreck, a fire, or a gift, I see the sex/gender complex, and religious turmoil surrounding it, as something vulnerable, true, and living, like a baby who needs to be held and carried. This word image is from Buddhist teacher Thich Nhat Hanh, who says this of anger and other difficult emotions. "Embrace your anger with a lot of tenderness. Your anger is not your enemy, your anger is your baby."[4]

The baby may laugh or cry or scream; he may make us feel joyful, tired, enlivened, or depressed. We expect a range of behaviors, and a range of responses, at various times. We hope the baby will eventually grow up and not need us anymore. Perhaps in future decades, we will find enough harmony regarding sex/gender so we won't need to address it with such intensity.

When we treat the sex/gender domain as something vulnerable, true, valuable, and living, we ask questions other than the binary questions (Is homosexuality right or wrong? Which side are you on?). We ask new questions, like those we'd ask about a baby we love. How are we holding it? How are we carrying it? Is it maturing and doing alright? When we hear it cry, we respond with the vigilance of a mother, discerning the need of the moment, mobilizing for right response. We expect to do this constantly for the foreseeable future, and see it as honorable, dignifying, loving work.

THE NARRATIVE ARC OF CONFLICT

Conflict is often described as an unfortunate end to a story—". . . and conflict ensued." As conflict resolution expert Bernard Mayer describes, "Somehow, to say that we are in conflict is to admit a failure and to acknowledge the existence of a situation we consider hopeless."[5] However, just as a baby's life has a trajectory, conflict itself has a narrative arc: a beginning, middle, and end. It

---

4. Hanh, *Anger*, 27.

5. Mayer, *Dynamics*, 3.

doesn't need to be the end of the story. It can be part of something larger.

In my family, for example, I notice that we have many conflicts every day. Amongst mother, father, three boys, and a cat, we tangle frequently: "Can I watch TV? He hit me! I don't want to! But Daddy said I can!" And the cat? "Food? Food? Food?" She never quits.

Something sparks a disagreement. It gets expressed and navigated with various techniques including clear speech, lies, manipulations, sweet pleading, anger, or sullenness. Sometimes power settles it, sometimes an appeal to rights, and sometimes a negotiated compromise. Sometimes the cat just needs to go outside for a while. Sometimes it ends easily, emotions de-escalate, and happiness is restored. Other times we need to talk about what happened and repair damage to relationships. Sometimes we have to wait a few hours to even do that.

I used to see conflict as an intrusion or a disruption; in short, as an avoidable problem. But now, after seeing so many small, daily conflicts and the way they strengthen our overall skill in relating to one another, I've realized that conflict is just one of the things we do together. It's something that happens often between people who love each other and are living close together, with shared goals and purposes. We can forever increase our skillfulness.

Religious conflict over sex and gender is like this, except so much more complicated. We don't have the intimacy of family. Issues are aired in extremely large church or denominational communities that include many strangers, or even just out in the open air of the Internet. The historical baggage we bring is immense: older concerns such as divorce and remarriage, premarital chastity, abortion, and women's roles are all still simmering, much of it not settled to anyone's satisfaction. Additionally, homosexuality very quickly touches on deep theological concerns about the nature of Christian unity, the authority of Scripture, and our ability to know the will of God.

This conflict is complex and ongoing, with very high stakes. We can discern at least three major dimensions, or domains, of concern: cognitive, emotional, and behavioral.[6] First, in the cognitive domain, are thoughts and perceptions. Here, we discuss what we think and believe, and why. Whether it is formal theology and ethics, or informal conversation within a family, church, or group of friends, there is great unrest and disagreement among believers in how they perceive the issues, how they evaluate sex/gender realities on an ethical or normative level, and how to exegete Scripture, apply it to our context, and think theologically about sex, sexuality and gender.

Secondly, feelings and personal experience exist in the emotional domain. Personal experience is given increasing authority, especially the personal experiences of LGBTQ persons. Many Christian LGBTQ people, and plenty of heterosexuals as well, feel deeply wounded—even abused—by religion. Their stories are intense and moving, and call for great empathy. It is extremely difficult to cultivate adequate listening skills, and even to muster the stamina to stay present to stories that call out a pastor, a church, or the entire religion. The Internet provides an open space for anyone to tell their story in a video, blog, or post, but this raises the challenge of learning how to read and listen, and whether and how to respond, to intense, highly personal and emotional stories that fly by on a social media feed, or that appear as a forward in an overloaded email box. It's also difficult to hear, or even access, stories from all relevant perspectives.

The third domain is behavioral, which includes both personal and corporate actions, including church or denominational policy-making, and policy-making and law in society. Here, conflict is more formal, with wins and losses measured in votes, policies, or freedoms. Frameworks often collide; what is seen by a religious institution as a matter of religious liberty may be seen by the courts as a matter of human rights, or civil rights. What is seen as theologically necessary by a denomination may be seen as discriminatory in the eyes of the law.

Conflict within each of these domains is deep and complex, and becomes increasingly so when all domains are at play

6. Ibid., 4.

simultaneously. In the midst of a denominational gathering, for example, where formal process governs speech and decision-making, a group of sexual minorities and advocates protest outside the doors, using emotional language and personal narrative to assert that their point of view matters because of their personhood and lived experience. A clash between the emotional domain and the behavioral domain is at play, and not easily resolved. The cognitive work of theology is carried on by scholars who keep conversation with one another across centuries, through careful study of literature. A denomination may make a decision that creates untenable boundaries for theologians working within that tradition, predetermining the intellectual conclusions those scholars must reach, should they wish to remain within the group. Such clashes between behavioral and cognitive domains are deeply painful.

Often there is no resolution that can satisfy everyone involved; if there were, it would have been found long before things intensified. Sometimes leaders work to minimize damage, and sometimes to transform conflict toward something other than its worst possible end. Conflict is a massive challenge—discerning when to avoid and when to engage, and how, both as individuals and as corporate bodies.

SOCIAL AND RELIGIOUS CHANGES THAT INTENSIFY CONFLICT

Some of the best fiction adventures involve shape-shifting, invisibility cloaks, portkeys, or transport into other times or dimensions. You think it's one thing, but it turns out to be another. That makes for a good story. Periods of rapid social change are like this—just as you get a grasp on what is happening and how you'll respond—poof, things change. It's a bird . . . no, now it's a plane . . . and now it's a what?

Recent social and religious changes offer both challenges and opportunities. They are the context of current conflicts, and they also sometimes trigger or intensify conflict. At the same time, wise leaders will seize opportunities to grow the seeds of conflict transformation. Changes bring new opportunities, and challenges as well, and both can provide impetus for new theology, ethics, church practice, and social engagement. This perspective portrays society and religion in a relationship of mutual influence, with some changes originating more in society, and others more in religion. To zoom out even further, an anthropological perspective emphasizes holism, the principle that all parts of human life are interconnected. Economics, politics, kinship and family, education, religion, and all other domains of human existence are interlinked, and while we can't predict or control the nature and rate of change, we can expect change in one domain to have influence in others.

1. Sexual Identity as a Social Category

Traditionalists only began to respond to the social reality of homosexuality in the mid-twentieth century. Traditional views of premarital chastity followed by fidelity within a male-female marriage certainly predate this time, and the sodomy paradigm implied and foreshadowed anti-homosexual theology and praxis, but it is important to realize that traditionalists, and progressives as well, have only been putting words, labels, evaluations, and theologies to the specific reality of sexual identity for less than a hundred years.

To offer an example, I think it's safe to say that my grandfather, a Baptist minister born in 1908, wasn't heterosexual. He wasn't straight, either, nor homosexual, gay, or queer. He couldn't have been, because those labels were not readily available in his context. He probably saw himself as a Christian married man: religion, marital status, and gender were the social categories that made meaning of what we now call sexual identity. Being a man married to a woman wasn't *straight*; it was just normal, that is, fitting with a taken-for-granted cultural norm. People of non-normative sexuality certainly existed, but their labels varied: invert, urning, homogenic, adhesive, and over time what became the dominant one, homosexual.[7]

---

7. Wikipedia contributors, "Terminology of Homosexuality."

I asked my parents, born in the 1940s, if they remember becoming heterosexual, and they do. They remember gay activists from the 1960s talking about sexuality, announcing their presence and demanding rights. They remember realizing, "If that's gay, then I guess I'm straight." For me, however, born in 1972, sexual identity labels were a taken-for-granted part of my world, like religion and gender were for my grandpa.

Accordingly, it wasn't until the 1970s or so that many churches and Christian organizations developed policies and language that prohibited homosexual behavior. The language, and the policies themselves, were responsive to new social changes. In effect, organizations said, "If that's gay, then I guess we're straight." These anti-gay policy approaches are certainly consistent with earlier centuries of pro-marriage and sexually conservative theology and practice, but their framing, their words, and their negativity (being anti-), and the meaning of behavioral prohibitions in a cultural context that links behavior and identity, was new.

The widespread recognition of sexual identity as existing—an important part of human life that warrants a social label and role— was robust by the mid-twentieth century. Christian responses to sexual identity are not "traditional," timeless, or spanning the entire Christian history seamlessly: this is not possible. Contemporary responses may be consonant with Christian tradition, but they are new framings, new wordings, new conceptualizations, that fit with a new social context.

2. Reduction of the "Abhorrence Factor"

Traditionalists often believe their theology and views are derived only from the Bible, and it may be challenging to see or accept the strength of social influence on belief. Anti-gay theology is certainly grounded in an interpretation of Scripture, but it has also been supported by instinct, enculturation, and lack of exposure. Being straight just seemed right and normal, and Scripture easily supported these views. In this view, it seems that God created the good and the normal, and we recognize that creational intent in what seems most normal and natural to us.

Differential religious and social treatment of same-sex attracted persons no longer seems intuitive or obvious to many people, including even those who believe the Bible clearly forbids same-sex practice. More heterosexuals have personal, friendly, and family-based interactions with LGBTQ persons, and nearly everyone in United States society has extensive media exposure to sympathetic LGBTQ characters and narratives. This results in painful tensions, expressed to me by one reader, "On an intellectual/theological level, I think homosexuality is wrong. But my heart/emotions lean toward acceptance."

When theology and morality have strong cultural supports—that is, when people in society at large are enculturated to believe and value what Christianity also promotes—beliefs and practices seem obvious and natural. When social supports for belief give way, the church must uphold these norms on its own. Christians may develop internal plausibility structures, supporting their distinctive beliefs and lifeways. This is often successful; for example, Christians continue to practice the Sabbath, uphold pre-marital chastity, and attend Bible studies, none of which have broader cultural support.

Other times, the church shifts to accommodate new social norms, as has happened with twentieth-century social realities such as shopping on Sundays, divorce, wives out-earning husbands, and mixed-race marriage. Christians even adjust theology and morality, finding that the heart of faith and the Christian tradition remains strong, and wasn't tied to certain issues in the way that had been believed.

3. Same-Sex Marriage

What will it mean for Christians to be pro-family and pro-marriage in a society that offers same-sex marriage? Christians are known for promoting marital and family stability in a pluralist society; that is, for families who are not Christian. Gay marriage expands the issue beyond desire for genital/erotic pleasure (not that it ever was so limited for LBGTQ persons themselves). It's about children, and financial stability, and support in aging, and caregiving, and being part of a neighborhood and community.

Conservative Christians have not yet reconciled an anti-homosexual ethic with a pro-family ethic, nor have they reconciled how to incorporate Christian gay families who wish to be part of the church, or same-sex married couples who convert. Some encourage converted same-sex marital partners to stay together for the sake of parenting, but to practice permanently celibate marriage. An elder in such a church once said to me, "We can't ask them to undo what they've already done, and we can't break up a family, but we can require them to stop the on-going sin of sexual intimacy." Some acknowledge the marriage as a civil union, but do not recognize it as religiously valid and would not perform or bless the marriage. Others allow certain kinds of church participation, but exclude those that would show the gay family to be a legitimate lifeway.

While these approaches honor traditional theology, they simply do not recognize the dignity or legitimacy of the gay family, nor do they meet the Golden Rule standard, treating other families in the way one wants one's own family to be treated. I've experienced this myself as a full-time working mother in an egalitarian marriage, when our children were very young and my husband scaled back his career to be home with the children for their preschool years. We had three babies within two years, and were fatigued all the time. Just one person made this comment to me, but it made a strong impression, and seemed to articulate the vibe of the broader community. This person had emphasized numerous times that the godly path would be for me to be a stay-at-home mom, and with sincere concern he advised, "You can do it your way or God's way. Of course it's hard when you do it your way." He meant it as a kindness, but it didn't feel kind. We've shifted to find Christian communities that support what we've come to believe is the best way for us to live and raise our family. Remaining in communities where the entire framework of our adult lives isn't valued, and where our children would learn that their family is second-best, would be, for me, religious masochism.

Pastor Caleb Kalenbach was raised by two gay parents (after his parents divorced, his mother lived with a lesbian partner, and his dad as a single gay man).[8] As he grew up, he found a relationship with Jesus and a calling to become a pastor, and has stayed in relationship with both parents even while preaching and practicing a conservative Christian ethic. He brings a rich, loving, hard-won perspective to his congregation. In his book, *Messy Grace*, he offers a list of powerful questions for churches to consider.[9]

- Would you allow a same-sex couple to attend your church?

- What would the reaction be if two men were holding hands in the lobby of your church?

- Could a lesbian couple who attend your church also attend a parenting class that you're putting on (because their child is in your children's ministry)?

- Could an LGBTQ couple serve in your church? If so, where? Why or why not?

- Would an LGBTQ couple be allowed to go on a mission trip?

- What would your staff do if a LGBTQ couple came to your church wanting to be married?

- If a man who had a sex change to be a woman started attending your church, could she attend your women's ministry?

- How do you love and support LGBTQ teens who are in your church?

These are just a few questions that relate to holding the tension of a conservative sexual ethic and a pro-family ethic.

8. Kalenbach, *Messy Grace*.

9. Ibid., 164–66.

4. The Internet

Prior to the Internet, separatist religious communities were fairly removed from society, despite immersion in mainstream education, economy, and technology. The Internet and social media have reduced, or perhaps eliminated, religion's ability to keep adherents ideologically separate from society. Alternate views, persons, and voices are readily available to young people in their formative years, and religious groups and /or families are not able to be the sole, or nearly sole, voices of authority.

Additionally, the policies and practices of religious groups are easily exposed via Internet and social media. Public exposure of actions, words, and policies is often immediate, partial, and inaccurate, and can't be controlled by either speaker or recipient. This is a strong and constant institutional concern when articulating, defending, changing, or discussing LGBTQ issues and policies. Dissenters and reformers alike create new narratives, and air grievances to the world.

Prior to the Internet, conservative religious groups could "come out from among them and be separate," living by distinctive sexual and moral ethics within the bounds of their group. They could filter the ideological, moral, and media exposure of their children, and they could raise children to expect to marry and stay within the group. This is no longer the case, and broad and instant access to information beyond that which is regulated by religious authorities has created a new information environment that makes traditional sexual ethics regarding LGBTQ life less persuasive.

Three other social changes originate more within religion, but like the others, influence the interplay between religion and society.

5. The Decline of the Ex-Gay Paradigm

For traditionalists, the dominant practical response to homosexuality, for the second half of the twentieth century and well into this century, has been to help gays become not-gay. If homosexuality is volitional sin, then stop sinning. If it is a mental illness, go to therapy. If it is an addiction, twelve-step it. And in all these cases, seek a sincere relationship with God and with a church body, trusting that a deepened spirituality will assist sexual repentance.

The ex-gay paradigm has been challenged for years, with ex-gay ministry participants testifying to harm done, and to change not happening. Outside researchers have argued that ex-gay efforts seem to prioritize religious identity over sexual identity, not turn gay to straight. Anthropologist Tanya Ehrman spent a year doing fieldwork at New Hope, the oldest residential ex-gay program in the United States, founded in 1973 in San Rafael, CA. Still operating today, it is led by Frank and Anita Worthen, who have also provided key leadership to Love in Action and Exodus International. The ethnography closes with a scene from the graduation ceremony at the end of the one-year residential program. Erzen concludes, "No one at the New Hope banquet would have admitted to feeling heterosexual or having sexual feelings for the opposite sex. Their notion of change was a matter of faith and maintaining a relationship with Jesus and each other."[10]

She explains more generally:

> Critics of the ex-gay movement assert that no one changes their sexual desires, and the New Hope men would have readily agreed. To them, change is a process of conversion and belonging that is uncertain, fraught with relapses and some temporary successes. For many, years after doing a program, change remains simply a leap of faith or a belief that they are doing what God wants for them. Much more than immediate change, the men and women undergo a process of religious and sexual conversion bolstered by relationships forged in the program.[11]

This fieldwork was conducted in 2000, and as years passed, more and more people within the ex-gay movement acknowledged that "change" referred more to spiritual transformation than

10. Erzen, *Straight to Jesus*, 219.
11. Ibid., 218.

heterosexual conversion. Erzen quotes Bob Davies, president of Exodus for twenty-two years.

> We know behind closed doors that change is possible, but change is rarely complete. I know many men who are totally transformed compared to twenty years ago, but that doesn't mean that they never have a thought or a memory or a temptation or a struggle. It means that the struggle has diminished significantly. It means that for all of us, redemption is still incomplete.[12]

Around the same time, Stanton Jones and Mark Yarhouse, both traditionalist evangelicals, conducted a study of about one hundred highly committed Christians pursuing orientation change and found the same as Erzen, that heterosexual conversion is extremely rare. More often, people experienced partial change in orientation, or no change at all.[13]

The ex-gay paradigm collapsed decisively when Exodus International, the umbrella organization for local ex-gay ministries, stopped operations in 2013. It acknowledged the limits, and sometimes intentional exaggerations, of its approach. Former president of Exodus International, Alan Chambers explained:

> I am sorry for the pain and hurt many of you have experienced. I am sorry that some of you spent years working through the shame and guilt you felt when your attractions didn't change. I am sorry we promoted sexual orientation change efforts and reparative theories about sexual orientation that stigmatized parents.[14]

Certainly there are still proponents of the ex-gay philosophy, organizations that continue to offer reparative therapy, and individuals whose lives have been changed for the better because of it. Proponents of this philosophy, including organizations and individuals previously affiliated with Exodus International, have

12. Ibid., 219.

13. Jones and Yarhouse, *Ex-Gays?*.

14. Lovett, "After 37 Years."

reorganized with the Restored Hope Network.[15] However, this model for life and ministry is now positioned as a less-than-plausible paradigm, one that is in defensive, rather than dominant, position within even traditionalist religious spheres.

6. Increasing Internal Pluralism in Churches

In the past, it seemed there was general consensus regarding the question, "Do you think the Bible says homosexuality is a sin?" within a given church or Christian organization, whether traditional or progressive. Minority thinkers functioned as their name implies, either keeping quiet, leaving, or promoting reform.

Today, views are rapidly changing, within groups and even within an individual, or carried with ambivalence and tension. For example, the "head" belief that the Bible says homosexuality is wrong is held in tension with "heart" compassion and lived experience with gay persons as friends, co-workers, neighbors, or family members. The view that the Bible validates marriage only between a man and a woman butts up against democratic values of inclusion and respect for law. The view that homosexuality is a sin is counterbalanced by the value of non-discrimination and human rights for all persons. The political frame of religious freedom, favored by traditionalists, contrasts with the frame of civil rights and justice, and it isn't always clear which frame is most important when addressing a given issue.

In traditionalist organizations, policies uphold a prior conservative consensus, but the populace has a broad range of views, which creates difficulties for legitimation and implementation. Such policies include euphemistic language that no longer seems clear (e.g., "gay behavior" or "homosexual activity"), and qualifications for leadership and employment and other institutional rewards that are grounded in sexual orientation. Attempts to distinguish between behavior and orientation are no longer intelligible; that is, judgments about gay "behavior" are understood to

15. Restored Hope.

be judgments against identity. Policies that aren't supported by strong consensus, and that are cast as discriminatory in the eyes of society's laws, are harder to defend, and increasingly face pressure from protest groups, internal dissent groups, and alumni groups.

7. Anti-Homosexuality Policies Shifting from Symbol to Practice

To honor marriage as between only a man and a woman, or to offer leadership/employment only to heterosexuals, or to list disciplinary procedures for same-sex behavior means one thing when there are very few LGBTQ persons out and advocating for equality within the community. In communities where sexual/gender minorities live as marginalized minorities, anti-homosexual policies serve mostly symbolic purposes. They remind the community of its boundaries, affirming those within, marking those without, and reminding internal minorities of their place.

Today, the increasing presence of LGBTQ persons who desire equality pushes organizations to put these symbols to work. Churches must decide whether or not a specific LGBTQ person can be in leadership, or on the worship platform, or teaching children. They draw finer and finer distinctions about gay identity, orientation, and practice, with certain combinations deemed morally acceptable and others not. At Christian universities and seminaries, administrators must determine and articulate precisely which behaviors LGBTQ students may not engage in: sex (which behaviors constitute "sex," and is it different for heterosexuals, lesbians, bisexuals, or gays?), dating, flirtation or public romantic contact (what is it, and who determines whether or not an interaction has romantic intent?). Pushed by federal requirements, institutions are just beginning to determine what constitutes right treatment of transgender or transsexual students, treatment that both respects civil rights and honors the institution's religious tradition and commitment.

In a society where sexuality-based discrimination is considered increasingly unacceptable, efforts to put taken-for-granted boundary markers into practice easily appear to be bizarre and draconian efforts of strangely sex-obsessed sexual conservatives. Policies that once served a relatively passive boundary-marking purpose are now pushed beyond their original purpose, now needing to actively monitor behaviors.

MORAL AND RELIGIOUS CONFLICT

Such is our context, and such is our conflict. All these changes trigger a shape shift, a set of interrelated and rapid social changes that have the collective effect of diminishing the credibility of a treasured traditional religious paradigm. These changes also provide the contours, or the context, and sometimes the trigger points, for the conflicts we face.

This anthropological approach highlights the mutual interplay between religion and society, noticing and naming new tensions that emerge due to social change. Determining the truth value, or biblical standing, of our beliefs, and how and when to put them into practice requires more than social observation. Right response requires the best of our intellectual and spiritual wisdom, and may well require more conflict engagement skills that we have yet developed. Like the honeysuckle vines in my backyard, it's a tangle. Things choke each other. It's hard to find the roots. You'll get scratched and poked. Progress will be slow.

Moral and religious conflicts are often categorized as difficult conflicts, even intractable. Difficult conflicts are those that seem to take on a life of their own and that result in mutual alienation, contempt, and atrocities such as suicide, broken families, and divided institutions. Certain social factors contribute to intractable conflict, and unfortunately, religious conflicts over LGBTQ issues exemplify many of these factors.[16]

- Periods of rapid, substantial social change.

- Compromised institutions.

16. Coleman, "Intractable Conflict," 534.

- Issue constricted to a binary framework.

- Issues touch on core concerns such as truth, morality, and beliefs.

- Polarized collective identities.

- Involvement of unconscious needs and defenses.

- People feel triggered toward humiliation, rage, loss, and deprivation.

- Conflict engaged multiple parties at multiple levels of society or institutions.

- Individuals and communities experience trauma, including loss of life and/or dignity.

- Fractured trust.

- Intergenerational perpetuation.

After listing these factors, conflict resolution expert Peter T. Coleman says the greatest hope for difficult conflict is preventing and averting it. Unfortunately, that ship has sailed.

There is also great potential for healing work, but only after the active conflict and trauma have ended. We're not there yet; we're in the midst. Unfortunately, when conflict is active, religion often pours fuel on the fire.[17]

This is a religious conflict. But is that all it is?

This is a moral conflict. But is that all it is?

If it is, God help us. No, let me put that more strongly. If this is entirely a religious and moral conflict, then we are doomed.

In the words of sociologist Peter Berger, "Religion is the establishment through human activity, of an all-embracing sacred order, that is, of a sacred cosmos that will be capable of maintaining in the ever-present face of chaos."[18] Various academic disciplines and Christian traditions would define it somewhat differently, but the important thing to note is that religion is not the same as God.

---

17. Ibid., 599.
18. Berger, *Sacred Canopy*, 51.

We are not called to worship it. It is not perfect. Our eternal fate is not in its hands.

In a social science view, religion is a human domain. In it, humans craft rituals and spaces in which humans can come in tune with the sacred. Though it may be couched in heavenly language, religious conflict is often about earthly things: institutions, ideologies, power, and money. What is the cost if we don't comply with federal regulations? What is the relationship between church and state, and how can we fight for what is rightfully ours? Who can be a member here, a leader, on the payroll? Who's in? Who's out? Who gets to say?

The stakes in religious conflict include group boundary maintenance, and religion's place in the modern world, jostling for both cooperation and autonomy alongside politics, family, education, and other social institutions. Such negotiations are often necessary, but they easily turn ugly, tolerate or promote violence, and distract religious people from the deeper purposes of religion, such as proclaiming the reality of an all-embracing sacred order. When things turn ugly, and when religion and God have been fused, people lose faith, leave their churches, and sometimes abandon the spiritual dimension of life altogether. In this framework, God is easily blamed for religion gone wrong. Drawing clear distinctions, and clear connections, between the earthly, human work of making religious institutions and the presence of the Divine in our lives is essential during conflict, for preserving both people's faith and institutional health.

Morality is part of religion, the teachings that involve "principles concerning the distinction between right and wrong or good and bad behavior."[19] Surely people define this somewhat differently, as well, but the important point is the same as for religion: morality is not the same as God. It does not save us. We are not called to worship it, or to put it at the center of our lives. It does not determine our eternal fate.

Moral conflict is about how humans perceive God as defining right and wrong. What does the Bible say about homosexuality?

19. Oxford Dictionary, "Morality."

Is it right or wrong? Is lifelong celibacy required? What does God think? Who can tell us what God thinks? How shall we deal with the immoral?

Moral conflict polarizes. People identify with their positions, and the stakes involve truth, goodness, and deeply held values. Thus, moral conflict easily gets ugly, tolerates or promotes division, separation, and even violence.

Conflict over homosexuality is religious and moral. We inherited that, but we strengthen it when we think organizational process, proper policy, or institutional stability will save us, and save society. We strengthen conflict when we believe right morality will save us, that the way forward is to know the right, and do the right, and teach the right.

At its best, religion serves the life of faith. Religious institutions carry and hold forth the possibility of finding the sacred and living in tune with it. Religion shelters the vulnerable, repeats the stories of faith, and encourages worship, devotion, and service. As the book of James puts it, "Religion that God our Father accepts as pure and faultless is this: to look after orphans and widows in their distress and to keep oneself from being polluted by the world."[20]

When religion becomes an idol, we have to serve it. We have to placate or please it. We fear its disapproval. When the highest priority is institutional self-preservation, we find ourselves avoiding sacrificial decisions, drawing boundary lines in self-serving ways, and amassing power. We might never see that this is our priority. By virtue of the all-consuming nature of institutional leadership, it becomes increasingly difficult for well-intentioned and highly committed leaders to perceive deep flaws and to correct course, though from the vantage point of those displaced, marginalized, abused, or damned by the church, these challenges seem perfectly clear. Social theorists describe these processes as part of the nature of large-scale modern bureaucratic organizations. Though no individual orchestrates it, institutions seem to take on a life of their

20. Jas 1:27, NIV.

own, prioritizing self-preservation above persons, and distorting mission for the sake of survival and growth.[21]

When morality becomes an idol, we have to get it right. We serve our best understanding of God's will, instead of God's will itself.[22] We talk about "what God says" and "what the Bible says," which are power plays, in a sense, heaping divine credibility behind what can only be "what I think God says" or "what we read in the Bible."

Jesus both perfectly embodied the sacred and failed to meet moral and religious ideals. He broke important moral rules in certain circumstances, for reasons that made sense to his conscience and in his relationship with God. Jesus couldn't make it through the faith screen, the behavior rules, or the leadership bar, of his day. He exposed the limits of morality and refused to give us another law. We, however, can't believe that we can go forward without some structure, some guidance of right and wrong. We'll do it in a gracious way, so it isn't the same as the Pharisees, or Leviticus, not at all. Again, it's the nature of idols to blind us to what we're doing, though if we look from the perspective of the outsider, of those damaged by the rules that validate those within, it can be seen. These voices are hard to hear because in response to being marginalized and often actively silenced, they may be angry or rage-filled, or even take on some of the behaviors of their abuser.

Morality has its place; that is, rules of right and wrong that are legitimated with reference to the divine. Rules restrain people from doing bad things, even if they don't see them as wrong. Please, let's make moral rules against child sex abuse in the church. It's good and right to accomplish behavioral compliance, even when the perpetrator's heart is unmoved. But we must be honest about what moral rules can accomplish. They can achieve behavioral compliance, using divine power and punishment as motivation. Sometimes that is enough. But rules should be the exception, not the rule. The vast majority of the time, religion and morality

21. Weber and Eisenstadt, *Max Weber on Charisma*; Weber et al., *From Max Weber*.

22. Ellul, *Subversion*.

51

should be promoting the life of faith, true discipleship that stems from freely chosen devotion. No fear of punishment, no looking over your shoulder for the law enforcer. Just love, blossoming into mercy, forgiveness, gentleness, peace, and self-control.

If current conflicts are all about religion and morality, we're doomed. I don't think that's all it is, nor all that we are, but we must be ever vigilant against self-deception, thinking we are practicing faith when we are playing with religion, thinking we are finding God's will when we are finding and locking in our view of God's will.

MOVING THROUGH CONFLICT

We are trying to move forward through conflict, holding our fussy baby while we don't get enough sleep and we can't get anything else done. As Thich Nhat Hanh described, we are the baby. We are the one who carries it.

How do we move? Andy Crouch offers a rich metaphor for Christian cultural engagement, a distinction between gestures and postures. Gestures are movements: embracing, hitting, defending, opening, closing, listening, leaning in, leaning away. Postures are firm, fixed ways of holding oneself. When a single gesture hardens into a fixed posture, we diminish our ability to be responsive, wise makers of culture. Crouch encourages a posture of flexibility, one that keeps us ready and practiced with a repertoire of gestures. Flexing with a repertoire of gestures empowers us to respond to rapidly changing social conditions, and to different people in different churches, denominations, and contexts.

> The remarkable thing about having good posture (as my mother never ceased to tell me when I was growing up) is that if you have good posture, you are free to make any number of gestures. As we're reminded when we encounter a skilled dancer or athlete, good posture preserves our body's basic freedom, allowing us to respond to the changing environment with fluidity and grace. But poor posture—being bent into a particular position

from which we can never quite escape—leaves us unable to exercise a full range of motion. With good posture, all gestures are available to us; over time, with poor posture, all we can do is a variation of what we have done before.[23]

We move in a dangerous sphere—that of religion and morality—and there are idols at every turn. The idol of religion tells us to serve and protect our organizations above all else. The idol of morality says if we don't get it right, and live right, all is lost. We also move in a society where conflict behaviors are becoming increasingly volatile: litigation, guns, texts and emails used to avoid difficult conversation, on-line flaming, and important decisions made from within a deluge of bits of information and opinions. Here, among these dangers, is the life of faith and the people of faith, listening for the word of God, poised to respond as we believe we hear it.

Power

Conflict resolution experts say conflicts are often addressed through power, rights, or interests.[24] Recognizing these tools can help us appreciate and anticipate the limits of any of our moves, and broaden our toolkit of responses.

This is the most costly approach, which is why it is best used most sparingly. We can, and sometimes do, resolve matters around sexuality with power. The denomination decides. The parents decide. The church decides. Gay ordination here, but not there. Gay marriage performed here, but not there. This youth group curriculum, not that one. Worship leadership for these people, but not those.

This is the use of religious power, the power of institution, finance, status, and prestige. Power can settle some conflicts and accomplish some good, but the gains are always quite limited. We see these limits clearly when a greater power dictates what our

23. Crouch, *Culture Making*, 98.
24. Mayer, *Dynamics*, 34.

religious organization can do, that is, when government settles a matter with law. We see such limits most clearly when we are on the losing side of a power decision. But power does have its place, and should be used wisely by churches and pastors and boards, by teachers and parents and leaders.

Rights

Conflict is sometimes addressed with rights, which most often has to do with the rights that churches and church-related institutions have to express their beliefs in ways that are distinct from the culture. Engaging conflict by appealing to rights can be productive, but also has limits. It is easy to see how institutions and individuals can comply with law, but only to the letter of the law, ignoring its spirit. And it is easy to see that any group will not win all the time: sometimes you win, sometimes you lose.

Rights-based approaches to conflict are like morality; that is, law-based, behaviorally focused, and often very rigid. They produce winners and losers. Some good can be accomplished, but don't expect to move the spirit with the letter of the law.

Interest

Interest-based conflict resolution recognizes the competing interests of various sides, positions, people, or groups. Interest-based moves are more person-centered, and more about compromise and negotiation. Negotiation and compromise result in partial wins, partial losses, settlements, and agreements to disagree. It requires engaging the interests of various stakeholders. At the very least, this includes LGBTQ persons themselves, the Bible, church policy, government and law, LGBTQ family members and allies, conservatives, progressives, and committed church members not very engaged with this particular issue.

This bumps up against the idols of morality and religion, both of which are totalizing and pure. When multiple groups are valued and included, results will be impure. Impure does not mean evil or harmful or sinful. It means mixed, containing otherness, an alloy. Such impurity of policy and practice threatens the impulse toward purity, and this is good. Perhaps if all parties lose religious and moral purity, all stand to gain purity of heart.

Sexuality is a dimension of human life that runs deep. It can even be seen as running parallel to our spiritual lives. Spiritual writer Thomas Moore explains:

> Sex and religion are closer to each other than either might prefer . . . like sex, religion lies at the very base of experience and shapes the way we think about ourselves and our world. In religion, as in sex, we ask: Where do I come from? What is it all about? Where is it taking me?[25]

Like spirituality, sexuality brings joy, delight, and union. It also exposes badness, and in intimate marriages or friendships, people often discover their own strange, ridiculous, and damaging badness in the presence of another person. Sexuality brings opportunity for confession and repentance, self-reflection, and change over time. In both sexuality and spirituality we find joy, delight, and union. We find badness, strangeness, ridiculousness. We practice repentance, self-reflection, and change over time.

On a corporate level, as well, sex runs parallel to spirit. Both call forth deep and basic questions of faith and religion. What is Christianity: a moral system, a religious organization, a way of life, or something else? If it's all about a relationship with Jesus, then what do we do with these buildings, finances, payrolls, and meetings? Do we serve our best understanding of God's will, or God's will itself? How can we know what is good, true, and right? What is the meaning and value of the Bible, the church, a pastor, a congregation?

Moore continues:

> If we were to see through the games religion plays with sex, we might find significant measures of spirituality in our sexuality and sexual delights in our religion. We

---

25. Moore, *Original Self*, 106.

might discover that they are two sides of a coin, one defended against by making it excessively spiritual and the other by imagining it as purely physical.[26]

To return to our original question: who are we, and what are we doing? We're the people of God, having a long-lasting, deep conflict that touches on the ambience of life's basic mysteries. Rather than picking a posture, or a camp, and sticking to it come what may, and rather than trying to perfect, to purify, or to hold it all together for God, let's rehearse and hone all our gestures, all our ways of initiating and responding, and get them in shape for a challenging and long-lasting conflict.

This is not the conflict of war, of battle, or of the Apocalypse. It is more like the challenge of early infancy, when the most important thing is to feed and comfort your baby, even when you are fatigued and the baby's needs are unpredictable and challenging. It is hard—super hard—but we won't win by defeating, killing, or annihilating anyone. We win by holding, bouncing, walking, rocking, and using every loving and tender expression we know to soothe, heal, grow, feed, and nurture.

The writer of Ecclesiastes offers this wisdom:

> Sow your seed in the morning,
> And at evening let not your hands be idle,
> For you do not know which will succeed,
> Whether this or that,
> Or whether both will do equally well.[27]

We can't control outcomes, we can't control other people, and often, we can't even control our own words and reactions. There is no quick fix, no guaranteed result. As you move forward in your local context—your church, organization, work, family, and personal life—what questions animate your practice, captivate your mind, swirl in your soul, and appear in your dreams? I encourage you to find a question or two and claim them as your own,

26. Ibid., 107.
27. Eccl 11:6, NIV.

the questions you carry in this leg of your journey. Sow your seed without knowing which decisions or actions will succeed.

Your leading questions may be religious: What should the policy be? How much money do we need? What do we need to stabilize our organization? How can my church develop language, programs, and relationships that meet certain needs or challenges? What does organizational leadership require of us in this time?

They may be also about morality and rules: What behaviors are unacceptable within our group? What will we do with people who violate certain rules? How do we teach morality without legalism?

They may be questions of lament: How long, Lord, how long? How have we failed? Who is suffering?

They may be questions of discernment: What should we do now? And now? And now? What is the loving thing to do? What do we know? What do we not know?

And when you speak any of these questions, or any utterance at all, let it be as you would speak to your own baby. This conflict is our baby. We are the baby. We are the ones who carry it.

3

————

LEADING

This set of lectures concludes with a reflection on courageous leadership in sex/gender conflicts in the church. First we explored beginning—beginning with who you are and where you are, in the midst of a rapidly changing cultural context and a knotty complex of issues, the sex/gender complex. The second lecture delved into how to best perceive and frame the issues. Conflict resolution literature offers a valuable frame, one that makes visible this high stakes, multi-generational, polarizing conflict in which deeply held values and morals are at play. Thich Nhat Hanh's metaphor of a baby helps us see and hold conflict well, encouraging us to hold, nurture, and respond to it as we would our own baby. When it cries, stinks, or screams, we don't ignore it or resent it; rather, we quickly move closer, like a mother. We are the baby. We are the one who carries it.

And now we explore courageous leadership, considered through the lens of Romans 12:1–2, and through the lens of cultural anthropology. This is "offering our bodies as living sacrifices." This is "spiritual worship." This is working together to discern and to do what seems "good and acceptable."

Perhaps you rise to the challenge: like Joshua or Deborah, you were born ready. Perhaps you shy away, like Jeremiah or Moses. You're too young. Not much of a public speaker. No one follows you. You don't like conflict.

Yet I mean to include everyone, not only organizational leaders with titles and offices, and not only those who seem to engage conflict easily. I mean courageous living, having eyes wide open to what is happening, and who you are in it, and how you might make a difference. This is an invitation to consider how you are part of Christ's work of reconciliation.

> Therefore, if anyone is in Christ, the new creation has come: The old has gone, the new is here! All this is from God, who reconciled us to himself through Christ and gave us the ministry of reconciliation: that God was reconciling the world to himself in Christ, not counting people's sins against them. And he has committed to us the message of reconciliation. We are therefore Christ's ambassadors, as though God were making his appeal through us. We implore you on Christ's behalf: Be reconciled to God.[1]

This invitation is for everyone: to live the life of love. As Dumbledore often said to Harry, love is stronger than magic. Magic isn't mere fiction. We Muggles often practice it. Prayer—that will do the trick. Right living—God will surely bless us then. Perform the right spell, get the right result. True religion, the life of love, relies on the same practices—prayer, right living, spiritual formation—but performed with faith and rooted in love. Spiritual practices are not expected to produce a particular outcome, but rather they position us to wait in expectancy for the sacred to manifest.

At the end of the series, when Harry faced the choice of joining Dumbledore in death or returning to the Battle of Hogwarts, Dumbledore said, "Harry, pity the living, and above all, those who live without love. By returning, you may ensure that fewer souls are maimed, fewer families are torn apart."[2]

1. 2 Cor 5:17–20, NIV.
2. Rowling, *Harry Potter*, 298.

This call to courageous leadership is not to encourage you to become pastors or public speakers or policymakers, or to join the bureaucracy of your denomination, though if organizational leadership is your thing, go for it. Leadership in families is also important—that of parents, grandparents, older siblings, aunts, and uncles. Communities, friendship groups, neighborhoods, and workplaces all benefit from the informal leadership of mature participants. Leadership of your own life is at the core of all these efforts, living by your internal compass and listening to the voice of the Holy Spirit within.

This is the life of love: being awake, aware of sex/gender conflicts, and discerning about what right speech and right action mean for you in your context and in your sphere of influence, be that a national stage, a local church, your friends and family, or your own life. Know that the stakes are very high, and that you are positioned to help fewer souls be maimed (maybe your own), fewer families be torn apart, and to call those who live without love back to the Way.

START SOMEWHERE

Where to start? Let's return to my backyard, to those honeysuckle vines that covered the fence the length of my backyard. I could say I worked on those vines for six years. I talked about them. I trimmed the parts that were easy to reach. I googled "vines." But I never really got down to business, never plunged into the thick of it.

When I finally did, my first strategy was to hack away at whatever I could reach. As I did, I began to see its logic. The vines wrapped around metal in a certain way, and around trees in another way. Certain things grew under, and over, and around, certain other things. Certain things flourished in the shade, and others in the sun. It was always a mess, always a tangle, but it had a rhyme and a reason to it.

Start somewhere, with whatever is within reach, and expect to get scratched up. Look for the logic, the patterns, the predictabilities, in the tangle that is your local context. And don't just talk about it, wring your hands over it, and research it. Go for the roots, with intention of seeing better health and growth over time.

This lecture begins with something less important, and concludes with something vital. We'll begin with a landscape view of positions Christians take regarding homosexuality. I could spend all day trying to convince you that my position is correct, but I won't, because taking positions isn't the most important thing. The vital matter is the work of reconciliation, both what we do and what we don't do, that helps us hold and carry this conflict for the long haul.

TAKING POSITIONS

When I teach controversial issues, I often begin with a landscape. Whether the matter at hand is presidential elections, gender roles, pacifism, or homosexuality, we often spend our time confirming, assessing, and bolstering our own view. At least as frequently, we might stand back and look at the entire landscape, understanding other stances by standing within them for a moment, and seeing the world from the standpoint of an Other.

L. R. Holben is an Episcopal clergyman who developed this model. His book is nearly fifteen years old, which indicates that we've been straining past binary for some time.[3] He describes six categories of belief regarding homosexuality, categories that span from extreme prohibition to extreme affirmation. The goal is to look at both structure and movement in the model, with an emphasis on how traditionalists are shifting, moving past binaries, and changing in response to religious and social changes.

---

3. Holben, *What Christians Think.* Summary of Holben's views from Miller, "GayMatter." See also Hollinger, *Meaning of Sex.*

A Spectrum of Views Taken by Christians Regarding Homosexuality

1. *Condemnation:* Scripture makes no distinction between same-sex acts and same-sex orientation; both are condemned.

2. *Promise of Healing:* Through inner healing, gays and lesbians can move into a heterosexual orientation, though a struggle with homosexual temptations may continue.

3. *Call to Costly Discipleship:* Complete healing may not be possible for all gays and lesbians; faithful Christians who continue with a same-sex orientation will commit to lifelong celibacy.

4. *Pastoral Accommodation:* Committed monogamous same-sex partnerships can be tolerated (not commended or idealized) as a lesser evil (for instance, better than the chaos of promiscuity).

5. *Affirmation:* Gay and lesbian relationships can be affirmed as a positive good; not only heterosexual relations but also same-sex ones can achieve a self-transcending exchange of love.

6. *Liberation:* Justice insists that the heterosexual majority in the church not dictate to gays and lesbians what they can and cannot do with their sexuality.

I was raised in position one, though not rabid or hateful. That homosexuality was clearly condemned in Scripture, and even that practicing homosexuals were probably going to Hell, was just taken for granted and mostly never talked about. In young adulthood, the ministries of Focus on the Family and Exodus International influenced me to shift to position two. I attended Exodus conferences, and even encouraged a close friend to pursue orientation change, advice that offended her deeply and, for a time, ended our friendship. A variety of influences have moved me over the last fifteen years, and I now roam around positions four and five. These aren't compatible with each other, but as I described earlier, my spiritual energy is not devoted to taking and defending a position. I find more spiritual growth in mercy, compassion, curiosity, and long-suffering as I listen to various personal narrativesand theologies, and encourage individuals and groups of varying viewpoints toward the work of reconciliation, whatever that may mean given their view and their context. I often find that this stance pleases neither liberals nor conservatives, but I also find resonance of heart with people of many different "head" beliefs. Such resonance is, indeed, a treasure worth more to me than theological agreement.

In the following sections, I will describe traditionalist movement across and between positions two through five.

Healing From Homosexuality: A Paradigm in Decline

Position two offers what seems like a clear, biblical answer to the problem of homosexuality: You're gay? Don't be. Become straight. Get married to a person of the opposite sex. The promise of healing and heterosexual conversion has lost credibility from professional psychologists and scientific studies, and was borne out in the ending of Exodus International. The basic idea is that, for the vast majority of even highly-motivated people who pursue change, sexual orientation doesn't budge. It does sometimes more often for women than for men, but this is not usually in response to attempts to change it.[4]

Nonetheless, I've heard personally from numerous individuals whose lives were transformed through ex-gay ministries, including stories of sexual orientation shifting enough to thrive in a marriage to a person of the opposite sex. These testimonies and stories deserve to be heard and respected. I received deeply meaningful pastoral care and support through Exodus conferences, which were in my young adulthood one of the only places where sexuality was talked about so clearly, and where I heard women sharing frank and personal stories of sexuality and spirituality. The promise of orientation change was overstated, even intentionally,

4. Diamond, *Sexual Fluidity;* Jones and Yarhouse, *Ex-Gays?.*

and that needed to change, but I don't like the mockery of this position and its adherents that is popular these days.

Position two is still alive, but not alive and well. Traditionalists are increasingly abandoning position two and are looking toward positions three, four, and five. While some traditionalists have shifted to position one, some with meanness and some with kind intent, this is a minority move.

Morally Mandatory Celibacy: A Paradigm Bearing Great Weight

Position three mandates celibacy as the only legitimate expression of sexual holiness for a person of same-sex attraction. Without the promise of orientation change, conservatives are left promoting lifelong celibacy as the only possibility for holy living.

While studying the Bible is absolutely vital, study of society is equally important, understanding how people live out celibacy in various contexts. Anthropologists Elisa Sobo and Sandra Bell see celibacy as both a personal and a social practice, changing the social world through active engagement or through the witness of one's own life. For women especially, celibacy can be a radical social critique, rejecting patriarchy and claiming education and personal well-being. In their global scan, Sobo and Bell conclude that celibacy is, and must be, social.

> Individuals or groups who refrain from sexual activity are, in addition to creating themselves after a specific fashion, communicating something about themselves in relation to others and so about their own standing in society. They are also often engaged in constructing and disseminating a coherent commentary on the nature of social life and a set of philosophic statements about what it means to be fully human.[5]

The celibate, then, should gain a socially intelligible identity, one that benefits them, their family, and society as a whole. This

5. Sobo and Bell, *Celibacy*, 8.

reflects the Christian understanding that sexuality should be for something beyond the self. It could be a life partner, children, service, community, or family, but it deserves to be vowed, or promised, to a real someone or someones beyond the self. Christians seem to recognize the need to build more supportive communities for celibates and to make it a viable lifeway of positive engagement, not merely an unabating negation clothed in loneliness. This is a profound challenge, and one that won't be met fully in the short run, an important consideration when calling young people to celibacy in the wake of the demise of the possibility of orientation change. The even deeper difficulty, however, is the moral mandate.

A. W. Richard Sipe, former Catholic priest, psychotherapist, and preeminent expert on priestly celibacy, argues against mandatory priestly celibacy, saying that true celibacy is "a freely chosen dynamic state, usually vowed, that involves an honest and sustained attempt to live without direct sexual gratification in order to serve others productively for a spiritual motive."[6] A vow comes with restraints—both marriage and celibacy do—but the vow itself is freely chosen by the person living it. Sipe found that very few priests die virgins; that is, most learn about their own sexuality through experience. Many reject the ideal, even while remaining priests, while others come back to celibacy over and over again, eventually integrating it into a deep, true, and freely chosen way of being. The seventeen-year-old novice and the eighty-year-old priest are both vowed celibates, but what the vow means for each of them, and how they live it out in daily life, is quite different.

We Protestants "otherize" Catholics at our own peril; concerns around mandatory celibacy apply to us, as well, even more now that position two is in decline. Catholic reformer and former priest James Carroll warns, "Celibacy cuts to the heart of what is wrong in the church today."[7] This refers to neither celibacy as an ascetic discipline, nor sexual sublimation as a mode of holiness. These are beautiful practices, when freely chosen and lived out in a nurturing community. Mandatory celibacy, however, in the

---

6. Sipe, *Celibacy in Crisis*, 32.

7. Carroll, "Celibacy and the Catholic Priest."

absence of adequate social support, fosters distortions of power in both individuals and institutions that, in Carroll's view, is seen in abuse and collusion that protects abusers.

Traditionalists working from position three are putting tremendous weight on the stories of successful celibates, using these narratives as the only model for others with same-sex attraction.[8] Many of these celibates are relatively young, from early twenties to about age forty. Thus, people who have already experienced intense and painful religious journeys, some very recently, are now receiving affirmation and love by virtue of their commitment to celibacy. This affirmation is conditional, it seems to me, on their maintaining certain theological views and on maintaining celibacy. This is a tremendous burden, to prove the livability of an ideology by modeling a life of celibacy, especially given Sipe's research that indicates celibacy is a long-term process, one that requires intimate friendship, accountability, and various routes to knowing and coming to terms with one's own sexuality.

We should also hear and learn from the stories of once-celibates who abandon the practice and choose partnership. We should hear from long-term celibates, those in their sixties, seventies and older, and develop a realistic sense of how likely it is for someone who vows celibacy at age twenty to maintain it, or even value it, for the long haul. Such stories are often marginalized or silenced, individuals who had once been "poster children" for orientation change or for celibacy labeled backsliders or frauds, and the wisdom we could gain from their hard-won spiritual journeys lost.

We certainly need to hear stories and voices from people living out treasured theologies, but celibacy as a response to same-sex sexuality is only one story; that is, sincere Christians choose among numerous life pathways and theologies. Successful celibates are like successful non-contraception users: their lives are wonderful

8. Belgau and Hill, "Spiritual Friendship"; Hill, *Washed and Waiting*; Roys, "Wheaton's 'Gay Celibate Christian'"; Timmerman, *A Bigger World Yet*; Tushnet, *Gay and Catholic*; Yuan and Yuan, *Out of a Far Country*. For theology supporting this view, see Gagnon, *The Bible*; Hallman, *The Heart*; Hays, *Moral Vision*.

examples of holiness, but the fact that God has gifted a small number of people to live in such distinctive ways does not proscribe it, nor make it humane or realistic, for everyone else. Nigerian novelist Chimamanda Adichie says of culture in general, "The single story creates stereotypes, and the problem with stereotypes is not that they are untrue, but that they are incomplete. They make one story become the only story."[9] Missiologist Sherwood Lingenfelter writes beautifully about the danger of a single life script, reflecting on a how "one-size-fits-all" moral prescription didn't fit his family's experience. He asks, "Are we willing to do serious work with Christians of same-sex attraction on framing new scripts and new ideals for community life and mission . . . ?"[10]

New Paradigms: Bridge-building, Sympathetic Listening, The Third Way

Positions four, and five, and sometimes three, seem to me to be part of the strain past the binary, reflected in labels and language such as Third Way, dialogue, reconciliation, and bridge-building. Whether you land in three, four, or five, or even position two, you may resonate with new calls for reconciliation, bridge-building, sympathetic listening, or the Third Way. "Third Way" is not an organized movement or paradigm; rather, it's a phrase used to refer to moving past the binary, with a variety of approaches doing something other than strictly negating homosexuality or utterly affirming it. These paradigms go beyond infusing traditional theology with a kinder spirit. They reorganize major components of theology and praxis, creating new centers and margins.

One key move is reassembling the center. In these paradigms, personal relationship across deep difference and respect for LGBTQ experience are considered central, crucial elements of Christian praxis. Secondly, these approaches push the question, "Is homosexuality a sin?" out of the center toward the margin,

9. Adichie, "Danger of a Single Story."

10. Lingenfelter, "Gay and Lesbian Christians," 227. See also Lingenfelter and Lingenfelter, "A Fuller Family's Story."

retaining it as an important question of biblical exegesis and personal morality, but reducing its priority. This question, and the positions people take regarding it, fall to second, third, or fourth in importance behind priorities including relationship-building, sympathetic listening, and a "just Jesus" evangelism and discipleship; that is, inviting people to Jesus without requiring or prioritizing a change in sexual identity, orientation, or behavior.

Evangelicals are being encouraged to listen sympathetically to LGBTQ voices, support gay families in their communities, support gay marriage, and support other anti-discrimination policies. Often these encouragements include a message of respect for theological conservatives; many say that traditionalist moral positions and readings of Scripture need not shift in order to accommodate these rights-based and person-based moves for justice. This may not be a viable tension. In response to bridge-building and reconciliation, positions do often shift. New forms of openness and inclusion, such as support for gay marriage and family, or ordination, or removing anti-gay language and policies from organizations, are likely. This doesn't necessarily mean overhauling or rejecting biblical interpretation that prioritizes male-female marriage and procreation, nor rejecting biblical authority altogether, though for some individuals and communities it may. For traditionalists, it is likely to mean tolerating LGBTQ presence in the church and society much the way some tolerate women in leadership, divorced persons in leadership, or even mixed-race marriage. The conservative need not change his/her interpretation of Scripture and is free to share his/her beliefs, but does so within a society and perhaps denomination or local church that has shifted to tolerance, or even acceptance, in theology and practice.

This is not unlike conservatives learning to listen to women speaking from the pulpit—women with MDiv and PhD degrees, perhaps wearing pants or short hair or gold earrings. It is not unlike accommodating drums, iPhones, and coffee. It is not unlike the very recent lifting of bans against alcohol consumption at numerous Christian institutions. All these things were seen as offenses against God and against Scripture, as disrespect, or as just not right. Yet they happened anyway, and we made a way to keep worshiping, praying, and serving together. In hindsight, they may not even seem like a big deal; people easily project into the past the current view that some of these beliefs were merely cultural, not timeless biblical mandates.

WILL NEW PARADIGMS LEAD TO LICENTIOUSNESS OR MORAL RELATIVISM?

Cultural anthropologists honor cultural relativism, which views the world of the Other in context, from the Other's point of view. Cultural relativism posits that other ways of life make sense on their own terms, in their own contexts. Correcting ethnocentrism by adopting cultural relativistic points of view is the heart of our discipline. Our core practice is ethnographic fieldwork, which involves the anthropologist living in the context of the Other, learning by immersion, and coming to see the world from the vantage point of the Other, as much as possible. Anthropological analysis makes sense of its subject by moving between insider views (the culture under investigation) and outsider views (a scientific view), ultimately developing a rich interpretation of cultural life that neither entirely adopts the Other's point of view, nor objectifies the Other as an object of the scientific gaze.

Cultural relativism, then, emphasizes that human lifeways are relative to context. It is a powerful corrective to our strong tendency to interpret difference as weird, wrong, or flawed. Moral relativism is different and is, in my opinion, a bogeyman—an imaginary evil entity called upon to frighten people. Anthropologists are among the strongest proponents of relativism both as a vantage point and as a value that fosters respect for human diversity. Many anthropologists would say that particular moral concerns of a given religious group—such as alcohol, dancing, tobacco, billiards, or card-playing—are indeed issues of moral relativity. Rightness and wrongness do not reside in the acts themselves, but rather only in the minds of believers, and therefore they do not hold across cultural boundaries. This is not the conclusion drawn about all human practices, however. Anthropologists debate long and hard about how to address human rights abuses, environmental problems, and other challenges, particularly when human rights discourses and local notions of justice collide.[11] Anthropologists generally rely on internationally negotiated human rights discourses for making moral/ethical evaluations across cultural boundaries, not unlike Christians using Scripture or tradition as an authority that reaches across cultural boundaries.

Moral relativism exists as an idea, a frightening idea, but not as praxis. No one argues that child abuse, government repression, murder, rape, or other outright injustices are merely relative to culture, though in each case we could find individuals or groups who would find the practices to be just. As a whole, however, we find a strong human impulse to work together as a species, across differences of language, religion, and culture, to improve human well-being, including sanctioning and persuading dissenting persons and groups. Licentiousness, ranging from minimally restrained sensuality to criminal depravity, is and will be alive and well in most human communities. It is important to consider how cultural norms, family style, education, and law encourage or restrain such problems, but it is unreasonable to see morality and licentiousness in all-or-nothing terms. A single social change does not stand between social order and moral chaos. Humans find both ways to restrain evil, and ways to practice it, within all social orders.

With respect to homosexuality, these new paradigms of bridge-building, reconciliation, and the Third Way foster cultural relativism; they find ways of sympathetically engaging the world and experience of the sexual Other. This will not lead to moral relativism or licentiousness in general, but may well lead to a liberalizing of prohibitions against same-sex sexuality. This is because of what same-sex sexuality *is*. Comparing and contrasting homosexuality with two other social phenomena, pedophilia and race, will clarify.

11. Deal, "Torture by Cieng."

The Case of Pedophilia

Drawing a comparison between homosexuality and pedophilia is as offensive as comparing Black persons to apes. In both cases, it's important to continue exploring the comparison because of the very real historical consequences of wrongly drawn comparisons, and wrong views of the nature of things. It provides a powerful illustration of Genesis 2, the responsibility God gave to humans to name creation, and the very real consequences of faulty naming.

When my pastor went to prison for molesting boys in our church, I went to my youth pastor and said, nearly in a whisper, "I think he was homosexual." In my mind—in a college-educated Midwestern congregation in the 1980s—homosexuality and pedophilia were pretty much the same thing, insofar as homosexuals recruited boys into their ranks via pedophilia. A terrible idea, of course, but commonplace in very recent years and not entirely out of circulation still today.

This isn't the heart of the comparison, however. Consideration of pedophilia draws a strong distinction between cultural relativism and moral relativism. A culturally relativistic view of a pedophile involves drawing oneself into his context, and the context of sex offenders more generally, seeing the world from this vantage point. In the case of my pastor, the first impulse of many outsiders was to see him as a criminal. In the eyes of the law and of society, indeed he was, and he was incarcerated for a time. But that wasn't how he saw the situation, nor how he was motivated. In his sick double-mindedness he was, on the one hand, doing something devious that must be kept private. But he also believed he was doing something loving, reaching out to share true love and intimacy with children. Sympathetic listening, or bridge-building, with someone such as this involves seeing things from his point of view and beginning to motivate change from his starting point. This can even engender empathy. Therapists and other helpers often describe a true human connection, a humility, in seeing how they are not so different from even the most deranged person.

Cultural relativism breeds empathy and effective change by building a connection with a person or group, understanding their point of view, and if need be, moving both the self and the Other to a better place. Cultural relativism, then, is more effective than ethnocentrism, which means seeing pedophilia from only one point of view—in this case, a legal point of view. Punishing pedophiles with the power of law is necessary and important, but it treats only the external behavior and doesn't move the heart or mind of the offender.

A culturally relativistic view of pedophilia does not inspire moral relativism. No matter how deeply an outsider may empathize and see the offender's point of view, and all the mental and childhood brokenness that may have brought him to this point, the criminal act does not seem any less wrong, nor merely relative to a particular person or culture. This is not to say, however, that definitions of child abuse, sexual abuse, or even childhood itself, are natural or obvious.[12] Humans negotiate the boundaries of pedophilia or molestation; such laws and social understandings are social constructs, the responsibility of humans to make, teach, and carry forward in society. I remember also in the 1980s, in conservative religious contexts, hearing that child abuse within the church shouldn't be exposed to legal authorities because it is the business of the church. When I saw on the television news my pastor walking toward the jail in handcuffs, I wondered, *can a pastor go to jail? Can the government do that?* I thought pastors were perhaps exempt from law. I also remember the notion that kids bounce back, and may not even remember abuse, so it isn't that serious. Strengthening contemporary understandings of abuse—that it is very serious, and the responsibility is the offender's, and that it is a crime—is important work begun in the late twentieth century. We need to continue refining and passing on this message to future generations.

The example of pedophilia shows that cultural relativism does not lead to moral relativism. Deep understanding of an Other, appreciating and even stepping into the context of the Other, inspires

12. Lancy, *Anthropology of Childhood.*

empathy and compassion even for a repugnant cultural Other, but not necessarily regard or affirmation. Compassion may mean letting the Other be, and celebrating the distinctives of the Other, as we may do for a different language group or a new refugee group. It may mean calling the Other to account, asking for a shift in behavior or mindset, based on some standard of right and wrong (a religious standard, a legal standard, or a standard of common sense within a given culture). Different communities—religious, scientific, professional, national, or international—struggle to find common ground standards by which to make moral and ethical evaluations, especially one that will be imposed across cultures, but they do in fact do so.

The Case of Race

For many conservative Christians, drawing a parallel between homosexuality and pedophilia used to seem persuasive: both were totally and obviously wrong, and in fact, they may be one and the same. Today this comparison has fallen into disfavor, and not only because it is, in fact, false. Homosexuality and pedophilia are seen as different things, in their essence: one a state of being, the other a mental illness or criminal act. Additionally, the stigma of pedophilia—the "stink" surrounding it—is shared broadly by Christians and others in society, and it is intensifying as time passes. In contrast, the stigma of homosexuality is greatly reduced, is unevenly shared by Christians even within a local congregation, and is reducing as time passes.

Comparing homosexuality with race is common, a comparison often used to encourage civil rights for sexual minorities. In this comparison, gayness is a state of being: not a choice, not a volitional act. Like race, it just *is*. Persons deserve rights and equality around dimensions of identity that are mere givens.

With respect to race and ethnicity, the practice of cultural relativism has meant learning to see, hear, taste, engage, and cooperate with the cultural distinctives of Others. It honors the American salad bowl, not the melting pot. Broader and more intensive exposure to the lifeways of Others is generally expected to produce empathy and regard. Empathy and regard are the domain of equal standing in society, and empowerment, voice, and self-determination. This is not the compassion of outreach or charity, but the recognition of the equal dignity and strength of personhood of another group. Groups and individuals partner across difference as equals in society and the world, not in helper-client relationships.

LGBTQ is not like race in some important dimensions. First, race is constitutive of our society and economy, a legitimation for color-based slavery that justified European colonialism and provided foundational economic strength to the founding of the United States.[13] The social construct of homosexuality—the notion of desire-based sexual identity—is not as historically deep, nor as constitutive of our society. Additionally, the distinctions between same-sex identity, orientation, and myriad behavioral choices are not distinctions at play in discussions of race.

Despite these differences, however, homosexuality is very much like race in terms of how these social constructs play out in society. Increased exposure to sexual minorities in society and media has generated recognition and appreciation. Terrible misinformation (e.g., that race links to certain crimes, or race links with IQ, or homosexuality links to pedophilia) is exposed as fraudulent when actual members of these groups meet and form substantial relationships with those who hold faulty stereotypes.

Whereas bridge-building with pedophiles does not lead to moral revision, bridge-building with sex/gender minorities often does. Like encounters across racial/ethnic minority groups, deepened exposure reveals the humanity of others, the likeness between self and other, and exposure of ethnocentrism and misinformation about the other. The Other, who we had feared to be criminal, deviant, and dangerous, turns out to be "just like us" in many ways, and in the ways we're different, their differences are mostly interesting and enlivening. When a despised Other turns out to be a good person, perhaps even superior to the self-proclaimed righteous ones, this poses a problem for moral disapproval.

13. Smedley, *Race in North America.*

For some, revisionist interpretations of Scripture reveal affirmation where there had once seemed to be prohibition. For others, the text still seems prohibitive, but an exemption, or accommodation is in order. For others, the authority of Scripture shifts. The very humanity of LGBTQ persons, and the fact that they are already marrying and raising children and contributing well to society, means we recognize, not grant, space to serve in society and church, and let God sort out judgment for all of us in God's own way and time.

HOW LEADERS MOVE

Holden's framework helps us move beyond simple binaries: "homosexuality: yes or no," and see that Christians have been working with a more complex spectrum of views all along. Even these positions will change over time, and the plausibility structures that make one seem better than another will change as well. We need not place faith in our minds or our rational attempts to make sense of our world and our place in it. We make use of our minds, but let's not put our faith or trust in our ability to assess and take positions.

Taking the right position does not untangle the vines. Holding one's position despite pressure, or changing in response to pressure, doesn't untangle the vines. What, then, should good leaders do in response to this conflict?

Surely it would be foolish of me to offer a "to-do" list: "Solve Your Church Conflicts in Six Easy Steps," or "Top Ten Solutions for Sexuality-Related Challenges." Local contexts are idiosyncratic, individual lives are unique, and the issues are rapidly shifting, so no overarching solution, no advice from a book or speaker, will fit every situation. Nonetheless, I'd like to risk playing the fool, and offer a couple of "dos and don'ts" that may be drawn down into local contexts.

1. Don't Fix It.

Problems that can be fixed are discrete and often mechanical, like a faucet dripping or too much salt in the soup. When people are involved, they generally do not like to be referred to as problems, and they don't like being fixed. Even when the presenting issue is policy, or media, or theology, when it's about sexuality, it's about people.

Religious believers often presume that religion provides solutions to conflict: "Blessed are the peacemakers." But quite often, religion itself is the problem. On a global level, religion is one factor that often escalates social conflicts toward violence and even genocide. Religion touches on ultimate values and meaning, and as conflict resolution experts W. Barnett Pearce and Stephen Littlejohn describe, "The greatest problem of all [in religious conflict] is that each side is compelled by its highest and best motives to act in ways that are repugnant to the other."[14] It's hard to compromise on ultimate values.

Rather than being positioned as a disputant in conflict, religion can be constructive when it serves as a container for conflict, that is, holding disputing people in community and activating helpful values and behaviors. Conflict resolution scholars Beth Fisher-Yoshida and Ilene Wasserman put it this way: "The challenges of our times are first to find a way to bring people representing seemingly irreconcilable differences together, and, second, to create a process in which people are both interested and willing to find a path that allows the acknowledgment and expression of the other's viewpoint."[15]

Here are some practical things leaders can do when they find themselves in a tangle of conflict over sex and gender: Carry it. Shepherd it. Nurture it. Redirect it. Contain it. Make processes. Make incentives. Celebrate. Lament. Gather. Speak. Listen. Ask questions. Answer questions. Self reflect. Negotiate. Compromise.

14. Pearce and Littlejohn, *Moral Conflict*, 7.
15. Fisher-Yoshida and Wasserman, "Moral Conflict," 560.

Confront. Hold accountable. Break impasse. Frame and reframe. Make decisions.

But don't try to fix it.

2. Don't Think You Know What You Don't Know.

Well-intended fixing and knowing have, over the years, led to Christians and churches advising people with same-sex attraction in a variety of ways. In colonial America, a man with same-sex attraction could be put on trial for sodomy. He could be put in stocks or jail. In very recent history, and even at present, he might be encouraged to view heterosexual pornography to stimulate his heterosexuality. Or dwell on insufficiencies in his family of origin. Or accept medical intervention including lobotomy, castration, shock therapy, or aversion therapy. Or marry a woman and trust that things will change.

Do we really think we're going to get it right now? We don't know the origins of sexual orientation. We don't know the future of any given individual. We can't predict how spiritual discipleship, religious conversion, therapy, or life experiences will shape a person's feelings and orientation.

We do know a few things, however. We know sexual orientation is multi-factored, and so is gender identity. We know sex and gender identities, and gender roles as well, shift in response to social, economic, and historical context. Change is predictable, but the nature and direction of change is not. We know marriage and sexuality are different today than in biblical cultures, and in many ways: age at marriage, cousin marriage, plural marriage, high concern for reproduction that serves a patrilineage, views of rape and sexual violence, and women's political standing. We know we are called to live by the spirit of a living holy text, not to replicate ancient tribal or monarchical societies.

A Buddhist phrase advises, "Not knowing is most intimate."[16] Not knowing opens us up to faith, to trust, to walking according

16. Miller, *Momma Zen.*

to the light that shines only as far ahead as the next step. To put it another way, it's better to know that we don't know, and proceed accordingly, than to know with confidence that which isn't possible to know.

Let's spend more time on the "dos"—three of them.

1. Practice the Faith.

This is the "just Jesus" approach. Just call people to Jesus, just invite and nurture people in deepening relationship with the sacred, and see what happens in their lives. You don't have to be straight, you don't have to be chaste, you don't have to "get it right" before you can come to know Christ.

Fuller Seminary president Mark Labberton writes, "This is the good news: that God so loved the world that the gift of God's Son reorders and enlarges our hearts and our lives." We're called to "recenter our lives on Jesus Christ."[17]

Jeff Chu, a journalist who is a gay Christian, went on a church tour of America, asking his book's title question, "Does Jesus really love me?" He visited a spectrum of churches ranging from rabidly anti-gay to totally affirming, in a variety of denominations. In the end, he preferred churches that focus on Jesus and on worship and community, not on a particular view of homosexuality. Chu says that homosexuality isn't, and shouldn't be, the focus of such a church. What most deeply resonates with him is churches where people are encouraged to "bring their whole selves, not just their sacred stances but also their profane fears and insecurities."[18]

I'm a "Jesus in your heart" kind of Christian, so I resonate with this approach and consider it vital. But it's not complete; it lacks certain details. Once you start calling everyone to Jesus, what then? Does your church perform same-sex weddings? Are gay people in leadership or on the payroll? What about the bylaws, the doctrines, the compliance with your denomination? And what

17. Labberton, *Called*, 8.
18. Chu, *Does Jesus Really Love Me?*, 311.

about a person asking you, or you asking yourself, what does God want me to do with my sexual orientation?

These questions need to be answered, but they are the cart, not the horse. Put first things first. First is robust Christian practice. Our habits shape us. Groups of people are shaped by their corporate worship, gatherings, service, and care for people both within and beyond the group. For individuals, practices such as solitude, study of Scripture, sleep, exercise, eating, serving, working, and even housework, when done with attention to their sacred reality, shape us.

Homosexuality and related issues are not distractions that prevent us from doing the Christian work we wish to do. They are not problems that, if solved, would free us up to move ahead unimpeded. They are not fires, threatening to burn down our houses. They are part of our context: like the Internet and presidential elections and standardized testing, they just *are*. For the Hebrews following Moses out of Egypt, it was desert living, idols, and uncertainty about the future. For Jews in the time of Jesus it was empire, oppression, and maintenance of tradition. In each incarnation, the people of God worship, pray, serve, sin, repent, lament, and so on. Same life, same God, and this life prepares and shapes us to live in these very different contexts, and to respond or initiate, or take or receive leadership, over different social issues.

2. Focus Individuals and Institutions Toward Psychosexual Maturity.

In the arena of sex and gender, new issues, new words, and new policies, seem to crop up by the day. If we keep trying to chase each snitch as it flies by, we'll fall off our broomsticks. We need an overall sense of what we're trying to do.

Richard Sipe says when it comes to sexuality, the church tends to focus on individuals as sinners, culprits, or problems when, in fact, individuals are sometimes expressing ecclesiogenic pathology—mental and emotional problems induced or fostered by church teaching and practice. It is "daunting to address a system as pathogenic or dysfunctional—the generator-participant in abuse." Nonetheless, these terms do apply to the church. Sexual perversions and compulsions are common "whenever healthy sexuality is repressed and denied instead of being recognized and practiced or joyfully and voluntarily renounced."[19]

One key problem in immature systems is a lack of a credible theology of sexuality. As a teen in a conservative church I remember hearing, "Just don't do it. What else do you need to know?" There's right and there's wrong. Showing further interest in sexuality was just a sign that you were doing, or plotting, something awful.

Absolutist morality and its breaches lead to the need to keep each other's secrets, denial in order to avoid scandal, and institutional moves driven by fear of exposure and truth. This is not institutional maturity; in fact, Sipe argues that churches often are sexual adolescents. They treat sex as taboo and titillating. They focus on intimate interpersonal behaviors, or on silence and secrecy. And even worse, they can be male clubs, with power held by men who practice immature sexuality, keep each other's secrets, and hold at bay the testimony and the influence of women and children.

I'm not meaning to paint all churches with a broad brush. I have been part of one horrific church, some decent ones, and some wonderful ones. But in my personal experience, my childhood church was the one where abuse would never happen—not here—and we were taught to trust the men in power whose godly authority was our covering. That's where the pedophile pastor molested kids for thirty-five years, with the broader structure offering enough denial and cover for him to continue. These problems continue today, over and over. People seem surprised that *he* or *they* would do something wrong, or that it could happen *here*. We seem to grant exemptions to people and institutions we trust, and are shocked, over and over again, when abuse occurs and when allegations of abuse are mishandled.

19. Sipe, *Celibacy*, 257.

How do we orient our institutions toward psychosexual maturity, in all dimensions of life: abuse, marriage, celibacy, dating, youth, adults, everything? How do we build structures that honor and shepherd people's complex sexual journeys? How do we get beyond institutional adolescence, excited and titillated by sex, experimenting with the boundaries, keeping secrets, focused on "do this" and "don't do this" without attention to the deeper life journeys of sexuality and spirituality?

While it's beautiful in the leaders and churches where it exists, as a generalization, it seems to me that we're not even close to having adequate theology, mature institutional support, or role models for believers seeking sexual holiness as LGBTQ individuals, but neither for singles wishing to be married, singles content with long-term singleness, divorced people, or even people in long-term, stable marriages. Sipe lists elements that support individuals in achieving sexual maturity: attention to physical needs, prayer, beauty, order, balance, community, service, work, and security. This advice would serve institutions well, also. In addition to policies of accountability directly related to problems, the more ordinary habits of community life are equally vital because they provide safety for all, even for the unfolding of relatively ordinary lives in relatively happy families. It is important, too, to understand the reasons why people fall away from their vows, and to learn by heart all the evil techniques used by perpetrators and colluding institutions to deflect responsibility, deny, blame victims, and refuse accountability.

Sipe goes even farther, recommending a code of sexual ethics for priests, a guide for sexual behavior for those who have vowed celibacy. It sounds contradictory, but his research shows that most celibates do not die virgins; rather, celibacy is a journey from ideal to internalization, from abstract to concrete, and for most, this includes sexual encounters or relationships along the way. He recommends a code that includes accountability, principles of informed consent, an obligation to respect the law, and an obligation to expose colleagues who break the law or breach informed consent.[20] This is a rich perspective that would cultivate sexual holiness, honoring celibacy even in the breach.

Most importantly, institutions need to see the forest for the trees, orienting themselves not toward avoiding scandal, avoiding trouble, or even toward proper morality, but rather, putting these goals in their proper place with reference to a more central center, psychosexual maturity, and even more central than that, the plain, ordinary, life of growing, active, maturing faith.

My own journey may serve as an example to broaden the issue out to all of us. It's not just about LGBTQ persons, or priests, or abuse. I see myself as walking two sexual journeys, interconnected but separate: female sexuality and marriage. Within my own mind, I live without a sexual identity label, but in society I am heterosexual, knowing that it is irresponsible to benefit from affiliation with a privileged category and not acknowledge it. But really, I see my sexuality as female, and see more in common in the sexual journey of my lifetime with all other women, than with heterosexuals as a category. For the last seventeen years I've lived within the constraints of my religious vow, marriage, which is to focus, or habituate, my sexuality not toward men in general, as heterosexuality calls for, but toward one man, James.

The church has supported these journeys in a variety of ways: we were married in a church, church members have supported us in difficult times, and we have always worshiped and served in a local church. With respect to sexuality specifically, I remember youth group well. We talked, or rather, the youth pastor and his wife talked while we sat there avoiding eye contact, about what is happening to our bodies, what do we do with these feelings, who can we touch, and how, and why. That was back in 1986, and while my questions have changed since then, there has not been such regular, communal, sustained conversation about sexuality past the teen years. As life has opened up into career, marriage, and child raising, spaces for forthright, self-disclosing conversation about female sexuality are even rarer than that once-a-year sex talk in youth group. The need for such conversation is often framed

20. Ibid.

in problematic terms (the very desire for conversation indicates a problem or crisis), and directed toward settings such as pastoral care or counseling.

Questions such as these are not indicative of crisis, or problems that need solutions. They are the deep questions of a relatively ordinary woman's life. What does it mean that I was born in this body? What is my way of being a woman? What is it to know and be known, to touch and be touched, to use my sexuality to generate new life, sustain intimacy, be an oasis of beauty and delight for one, and in another way, for the world? How do I carry disappointment, and loss, the death and life that only a woman's body can contain? How does my marriage handle the ordinary evil we inflict on each other—the meanness, the small daily torments? Are we doing alright—will we be alright together—and how would we know?

It's not just theology that I need, or a church that takes the proper stance on a given issue. It's friendship, companionship, women who have lived into their femininity, internalized the image of God, becoming more fully the specific person, the specific woman, God made them to be. I need married people who have lived their vows longer than I have, who have failed and lived to tell the tale, who will tell the truth about sexuality during early marriage, childbearing years, medications, sicknesses, distraction, work, unemployment, aging, and grief.

Reaching the right conclusion regarding the morality of homosexuality is far from the point. Sexual health and wholeness is a lifelong journey, for every single person, and it is not merely erotic; it is also about bodily integrity and health, prevention of sickness and harm, healing from trauma and abuse, and simply learning to be comfortable in one's own skin.

Those dominating binary questions are exposed, then, as inadequate. "Does the Bible say homosexuality is a sin?" and "How should Christians respond to homosexuality in the church?"

Those aren't the questions. They are questions within questions. The big questions about sexuality and gender are more like these:

How do my past, present, and future connect? Does my life have a coherent narrative?

Who am I, sexually, and who am I becoming?

What is my religious vow for my sexuality, and how do I live into it?

Who has lived a similar path, and will they share their story?

Who am I, in society's eyes? Who am I, in God's eyes? Who am I, in my own eyes?

Instead of separating people into groups according to what they want sexually, better to direct all persons toward spiritual and psychosexual wholeness; that is, human wholeness. This can't just leave individuals alone to discern what feels right to them. This is an obvious recipe for self-deception. Between the poles of institutionally mandated morality and isolated individualism lies community. A more robust process of moral discernment may include conscience, community, Bible study, historical study, and consideration of our global sisters and brothers. Such a process may require knowing, being known, and even not knowing in face-to-face communities of friendship and spiritual encouragement.

3. Cultivate a Repertoire of Conflict Resolution Skills.

Mennonite conflict resolution expert John Paul Lederach describes conflict as emerging from, and happening within, four dimensions: personal, relational, structural, and cultural. He recommends learning to perceive conflict, and then intervening to promote change at all levels through nonviolent mechanisms.[21]

This work is not a side interest for the few, for those who feel especially called to conflict work. Indeed, there are very few such persons, because conflict is so uncomfortable. Rather,

> . . . reconciliation is the mission, the organizing purpose around which we understand and see God's work in

21. Lederach, "Conflict Transformation," 52. See also Schirch, *Little Book.*

history. I believe that the way God has chosen to be present and act throughout history demonstrates a methodology of reconciliation. Our mission is to align ourselves with God, who is working to bring all things together, to reconcile all of creation and particularly a broken, estranged humanity.[22]

A framework for perceiving conflict can help leaders identify what is at play in a given situation—what within that is important, and within that, what is most important. What might be important? A merely cursory list might include the Bible, tradition, persons directly impacted by conflict, persons indirectly impacted, personal moral views, corporate moral views, compliance with law, and public relations.

Peaceful, nonviolent change sounds good, but is very challenging to put into practice. Because, ultimately, it's conflict. Because he said this and she said that. Because we could move forward easily if it weren't for, well, those other people in the conflict.

We can't control outcomes, and we can't control other people, but here are a few things we can do to maximize religion's capacity for peace-making, a capacity very easily bent toward violence and trouble.[23]

- Orient yourself and your people to a fair process, a way of being and living. If we remain oriented to outcomes and possible losses, reconciliation is less likely.

- Understand and name the conflict. In your purview, include systems, persons, the short and long term, the past, present, and future.

- Initiate and sustain constructive change. Let go of the expectation that change will be straightforward, timely, or consistent.

- "Ripen" and incentivize participants for constructive engagement.

---

22. Lederach, *Reconcile*, 145.
23. Adapted from Coleman; Fisher-Yoshida and Wasserman.

- Construct processes that will motivate disputants to come to the table.

- Train for crisis and trauma.

- Find and encourage the resources motivated toward peace in your environment.

Maybe this isn't your thing? Not your area of expertise? Join the club! Conflict is difficult and unpleasant, by definition. But each of us are part of today's conflicts over sex and gender, simply by being part of the church. It's in the air we breathe when we live as part of God's family. It's a challenge, but each of us have gifts to offer, and lessons to learn, in our spheres of responsibility. Be that leadership in a local church, a workplace role, or our place in our families, there is healing work to be done.

CONCLUSION

On the one hand, I see that simply *it is*. Homosexuality *is*. Lesbians *are*. Transgender people *are*. They just *are*. There is respect in merely recognizing the existence of social Others and letting them be. This may even be a form of prayer. Amen. Let it be. The church has put so much energy into moral judgment, and while there is a place for moral evaluation, there are true spiritual fruits left unripened: mercy, kindness, generosity, joy, and self-control, just to name a few. We could work on those for a few years, perhaps, or for a few centuries.

On the other hand, I see this complex of issues as a social conflict. It warrants the full range of conflict resolution theories and practices. We're not preventing conflict, nor healing after it is over. We're in the midst of it. Every religious gathering I've been to includes people of various stances, liberals and conservatives, people of various sexual identities, and people deeply wounded by religion. The way forward is together—all of us, together.

As mentioned in Chapter 2, this is an impure approach. Liberals may settle for less than what they perceive as justice, and may need to tolerate ongoing conversation about morality and the

Bible: conversations that are still alive and meaningful for many, even if not for them. Conservatives may settle for less than what they perceive as righteousness, or morality, with same-sex partnered people in their midst, even providing religious leadership.

This impurity is good. It is not the impurity of dirtiness; rather, of alloy. Alloys involve unlike things residing close together and mixing. Some parts are of greater value, and some less. Alloys are sometimes stronger, and sometimes not. They are sometimes more valuable, and sometimes not. You have to work with it, watch it, and adjust it.

Our inability to fix the problem of homosexuality, and our inability to know all that we wish to know, is not a problem; it is a gift. It is the fruit of Moses's anger, grinding down the golden calf for the people to drink. It restrains our idolatry, our desire to get it right and do it right by our own effort.

Antonio Machado's well-loved poem reminds us:

> Traveler, there is no road.
> We make the road by walking.
> . . .
> Traveller, there is no road
> Only wakes in the sea.[24]

We make the road by walking it, but we don't walk alone. The Way is lit, just enough, by the living word of God, the lamp for our feet, and the light on our path.[25]

---

24. Machado and Barnstone, *Border*.
25. Ps 119:105, NIV.

BIBLIOGRAPHY

Adichie, Chimamanda Ngozi. "The Danger of a Single Story." Filmed July 2009. TED video. Online: http://www.ted.com/talks/chimamanda_adichie_the_danger_of_a_single_story/transcript.

American Anthropological Association. "This is Anthropology." Online: http://www.thisisanthropology.org.

Beck, James R., et al. *Two Views on Women in Ministry.* Grand Rapids: Zondervan, 2001.

Belgau, Ron, and Wesley Hill. *Spiritual Friendship: Musings on God, Sexuality, Relationships.* Personal Blog. Online: http://spiritualfriendship.org.

Berger, Peter L. *The Sacred Canopy: Elements of a Sociological Theory of Religion.* New York: Anchor, 1990.

Blank, Hanne. *Straight: The Surprisingly Short History of Heterosexuality.* Boston: Beacon, 2012.

Bray, Gerald Lewis, and Thomas C. Oden. *Romans.* Downers Grove, IL: InterVarsity, 2005.

Brownson, James V. *Bible, Gender, Sexuality: Reframing the Church's Debate on Same-Sex Relationships.* Grand Rapids: Eerdmans, 2013.

Carroll, James. "Celibacy and the Catholic Priest." *The Boston Globe.* May 16, 2010. Online: http://www.boston.com/bostonglobe/editorial_opinion/oped/articles/2010/05/16/celibacy_and_the_catholic_priest.

Chu, Jeff. *Does Jesus Really Love Me? A Gay Christian's Pilgrimage in Search of God in America.* New York: Harper, 2013.

Coleman, Peter T. "Intractable Conflict." In *The Handbook of Conflict Resolution: Theory and Practice,* edited by Morton Deutsch, et al., 533–59. San Francisco: Jossey-Bass, 2000.

Crouch, Andy. *Culture Making: Recovering our Creative Calling.* Downers Grove, IL: InterVarsity, 2008.

Dawn, Marva J. *A Royal Waste of Time: The Splendor of Worshiping God and Being Church for the World.* Grand Rapids: Eerdmans, 1999.

D'Emilio, John, and Estelle B. Freedman. *Intimate Matters: A History of Sexuality in America.* New York: Harper & Row, 1988.

Deal, Jeffery L. "Torture by Cieng: Ethical Theory Meets Social Practice among the Dinka Agaar of South Sudan." *American Anthropologist* 112 (2010) 563–75.

Diamond, Lisa M. *Sexual Fluidity: Understanding Women's Love and Desire.* Cambridge: Harvard University Press, 2008.

Ellul, Jacques. *The Subversion of Christianity.* Grand Rapids: Eerdmans, 1986.

Erzen, Tanya. *Straight to Jesus: Sexual and Christian Conversions in the Ex-Gay Movement.* Berkeley: University of California Press, 2006.

Fisher-Yoshida, Beth, and Ilene Wasserman. "Moral Conflict and Engaging Alternative Perspectives." In *The Handbook of Conflict Resolution: Theory and Practice,* edited by Morton Deutsch, et al., 560–81. San Francisco: Jossey-Bass, 2000.

Foucault, Michel. *The History of Sexuality.* New York: Pantheon, 1978.

Gagnon, Robert. *The Bible and Homosexual Practice: Texts and Hermeneutics.* Nashville: Abingdon, 2001.

Geertz, Clifford. *The Interpretation of Cultures: Selected Essays.* New York: Basic, 1973.

Gerber, Lynne. *Seeking the Straight and Narrow: Weight Loss and Sexual Reorientation in Evangelical America.* Chicago: University of Chicago Press, 2011.

Gerson, Michael. "An Appeal for Patient Pluralism." *Washington Post.* February 12, 2015. Online: http://www.washingtonpost.com/opinions/a-call-for-patient-pluralism/2015/02/12/f9a636e4-b300-11e4-886b-c22184f27c35_story.html.

Greenberg, David F. *The Construction of Homosexuality.* Chicago: University of Chicago Press, 1988.

Gritter, Wendy VanderWal. *Generous Spaciousness: Responding to Gay Christians in the Church.* Grand Rapids: Brazos, 2014.

Gushee, David P. *Changing Our Mind: A Call from America's Leading Evangelical Ethics Scholar for Full Acceptance of LGBT Christians in the Church.* Canton, MI: David Crumm Media, 2014.

Hanh, Thich Nhat. *Anger: Wisdom for Cooling the Flames.* New York: Riverhead Books, 2002.

Hallman, Janelle M. *The Heart of Female Same-Sex Attraction: A Comprehensive Counseling Resource.* Downers Grove, IL: InterVarsity, 2008.

Hays, Richard B. *The Moral Vision of the New Testament: A Contemporary Introduction to New Testament Ethics.* San Francisco: Harper San Francisco, 1996.

Hiebert, Paul G. *The Gospel in Human Contexts: Anthropological Explorations for Contemporary Missions.* Grand Rapids: Baker Academic, 2009.

Hill, Wesley. *Washed and Waiting: Reflections on Christian Faithfulness and Homosexuality.* Grand Rapids: Zondervan, 2010.

Holben, L. R. *What Christians Think About Homosexuality: Six Representative Viewpoints.* North Richland Hills, TX: Bibal, 1999.

Hollinger, Dennis P. *The Meaning of Sex: Christian Ethics and the Moral Life.* Grand Rapids: Baker Academic, 2009.

Howell, Brian M., and Jenell Williams Paris. *Introducing Cultural Anthropology: A Christian Perspective.* Grand Rapids: Baker Academic, 2011.

Hunt, Mary E., and Diann L. Neu. *New Feminist Christianity: Many Voices, Many Views.* Woodstock: SkyLight Paths, 2010.

Irvine, Janice M. *Disorders of Desire: Sex and Gender in Modern American Sexology.* Philadelphia: Temple University Press, 1990.

Jones, Stanton L., and Mark A. Yarhouse. *Ex-Gays?: A Longitudinal Study of Religiously Mediated Change in Sexual Orientation.* Downers Grove, IL: InterVarsity, 2007.

Kalenbach, Caleb. *Messy Grace.* Colorado Springs, CO: Waterbrook Multnomah, forthcoming.

Katz, Jonathan Ned. *The Invention of Heterosexuality.* New York: Dutton, 1995.

Keener, Craig S. *The IVP Bible Background Commentary, New Testament.* Downers Grove, IL: InterVarsity, 1993.

Labberton, Mark. *Called: The Crisis and Promise of Following Jesus Today.* Downers Grove, IL: InterVarsity, 2014.

Lancy, David F. *The Anthropology of Childhood: Cherubs, Chattel, Changelings.* Cambridge: Cambridge University Press, 2008.

Lawrence, Brother. *The Practice of the Presence of God.* Grand Rapids: Baker, 1967.

Lederach, John Paul. "Conflict Transformation." In *Mediation and Facilitation Training Manual: Foundations and Skills for Constructive Conflict Transformation*, edited by Carolyn Schrock-Shenk, 52. 4th ed. Akron: Mennonite Conciliation Service.

———. *Reconcile: Conflict Transformation for Ordinary Christians.* Harrisonburg, VA: Herald, 2014.

Lingenfelter, Sherwood. "Gay and Lesbian Christians: Framing Questions and Clarifying the Debate About a Place in Church and Mission for Evangelical LGBTQ Youth." In *The Missionary Family: Witness, Concerns, Care*, edited by Dwight Baker and Robert J. Priest, 208–30. Pasadena, CA: William Carey Library, 2014.

Lingenfelter, Sherwood, and Jennifer Lingenfelter. "A Fuller Family's Story of Homosexuality and Faith." The Burner Blog. Posted February 2012. http://theburnerblog.com/sexuality-2/a-fuller-familys-story-of-homosexuality-and-faith.

Lovett, Ian. "After 37 Years of Trying to Change People's Sexual Orientation, Group to Disband." *New York Times.* June 30, 2013. Online: http://www.nytimes.com/2013/06/21/us/group-that-promoted-curing-gays-ceases-operations.html?_r=0.

Machado, Antonio, and Willis Barnstone. *Border of a Dream: Selected Poems of Antonio Machado.* Port Townsend, WA: Copper Canyon, 2004.

MacIntyre, Alasdair. *After Virtue: A Study in Moral Theory.* 2nd ed. Notre Dame: University of Notre Dame Press, 1984.

Mayer, Bernard S. *The Dynamics of Conflict Resolution: A Practitioner's Guide.* San Francisco: Jossey-Bass, 2000.

Miller, Harold. "GayMatter." *Interacting with Jesus.* Online: http://interactingwithjesus.org/gaymatter/spectrum.html.

Miller, Karen Maezen. *Momma Zen: Walking the Crooked Path of Motherhood.* Boston: Shambhala, 2006.

Moore, Thomas. *Original Self: Living with Paradox and Originality.* New York: HarperCollins, 2001.

Murray, Stephen O. *Homosexualities.* Chicago: University of Chicago Press, 2000.

Nanda, Serena. *Gender Diversity: Crosscultural Variations.* Prospect Heights, IL: Waveland, 2000.

———. *Neither Man Nor Woman: The Hijras of India.* Belmont, CA: Wadsworth, 1990.

Niebuhr, H. Richard. *Christ and Culture.* New York: Harper, 1951.

Ontario Consultants on Religious Tolerance, "Homosexuality in the Christian Scriptures." Religious Tolerance. Online: http://www.religioustolerance. org/hom_bibc1.htm.

Otto, Tim. *Oriented to Faith: Transforming the Conflict over Gay Relationships.* Eugene, OR: Cascade, 2014.

Oxford Dictionary, "Morality." Online: http://www.oxforddictionaries.com/us/ definition/american_english/morality.

Paris, Jenell Williams, and Rory Anderson. "Faith-based Queer Space in Washington, DC: the Metropolitan Community Church–DC and Mount Vernon Square." *Gender, Place and Culture* 8 (2001) 149–68.

Pearce, W. Barnett, and Stephen Littlejohn. *Moral Conflict: When Social Worlds Collide.* Thousand Oaks: Sage, 1997.

Priest, Robert J. "Unpublished draft." Shared with Jenell Paris. March 9, 2015.

Raman, Varadaraja. "The Heart's Reason." In *Einstein's God: Conversations About Science and the Human Spirit*, edited by Krista Tippett, 121–42. New York: Penguin, 2010.

Rowling, J. K. *Harry Potter and the Sorcerer's Stone.* New York: A.A. Levine, 1998.

Roys, Julie. "Wheaton's 'Gay Celibate Christian.'" *World.* December 11, 2014. Online: http://www.worldmag.com/2014/12/wheaton_s_gay_celibate_ christian.

Sargeant, Winthrop. "It's All Anthropology." *The New Yorker.* December 30, 1961.

Schirch, Lisa. *The Little Book of Strategic Peacebuilding.* Intercourse, PA: Good Books, 2004.

Sipe, A. W. Richard. *Celibacy in Crisis: A Secret World Revisited.* New York: Brunner-Routledge, 2003.

Slick, Matt. "The Word 'Homosexual' Didn't Appear in English Bibles Until 1946." Christian Apologetics and Research Ministry. Online: https://carm. org/word-homosexual-english-bible-1946.

Smedley, Audrey. *Race in North America Origin and Evolution of a Worldview.* Boulder, CO: Westview, 2011.

Smith, Christian. *The Bible Made Impossible: Why Biblicism Is Not a Truly Evangelical Reading of Scripture.* Grand Rapids: Brazos, 2011.

Smith, James K. A. *Desiring the Kingdom: Worship, Worldview, and Cultural Formation.* Grand Rapids: Baker Academic, 2009.

———. *Imagining the Kingdom: How Worship Works.* Grand Rapids: Baker Academic, 2013.

Sobo, Elisa, and Sandra Bell, eds. *Celibacy, Culture, and Society: The Anthropology of Sexual Abstinence.* Madison: University of Wisconsin Press, 2001.

Timmerman, Tim. *A Bigger World Yet: Faith, Brotherhood, and Same Sex Needs.* Newberg, OR: Bird Dog, 2010.

Tushnet, Eve. *Gay and Catholic: Accepting My Sexuality, Finding Community, Living My Faith.* Notre Dame: Ave Maria, 2014.

Vines, Matthew. *God and the Gay Christian: The Biblical Case in Support of Same-Sex Relationships.* New York: Convergent, 2014.

Weber, Max, and S. N. Eisenstadt. *Max Weber on Charisma and Institution Building: Selected Papers.* Chicago: University of Chicago Press, 1968.

Weber, Max, et al. *From Max Weber: Essays in Sociology.* New York: Oxford University Press, 1958.

Wiesner-Hanks, Merry E. *Gender in History.* Malden: Blackwell, 2001.

Wikipedia contributors, "Terminology of Homosexuality." Online: https://en.wikipedia.org/wiki/Terminology_of_homosexuality.

Yuan, Christopher, and Angela Yuan. *Out of a Far Country: A Gay Son's Journey to God: A Broken Mother's Search for Hope.* Colorado Springs, CO: Waterbrook, 2011.

Made in the USA
Lexington, KY
10 February 2018